CASH BOX CONJURE

HOODOO SPELLS FOR LUCK AND MONEY

MISS PHOENIX LEFAE

Lucky Mojo Curio Company
Forestville, California

✦ 2018 ✦

Cash Box Conjure:
Hoodoo Spells for Luck and Money
by Miss Phœnix LeFæ

© 2018 Phœnix LeFæ
PhoenixLeFae.com

Text:
Miss Phœnix LeFæ

Editor:
catherine yronwode

Cover:
Grey Townsend, National Cash Register Catalogue, Alissa Van de Vuurst

Illustrations:
Charles C. Dawson, Charles M. Quinlan, J. C. Strong,
Grey Townsend, and Unknown Artists

Typesetting:
catherine yronwode

Production:
nagasiva yronwode

First Edition 2018

Published by
The Lucky Mojo Curio Company
6632 Covey Road
Forestville, California 95436
LuckyMojo.com

ISBN: 978-0-9961471-8-7

Printed in Canada.

CONTENTS

DEDICATION

This book is dedicated to the root doctors, witches, wise women, and spiritual practitioners who keep mysticism alive. This book is dedicated to the people of Africa who were taken from their homes and families, carried across the seas, and forced into servitude. This book is dedicated to the folks who spent their lives working with roots to help their families, their communities, and their people find hope and chance. This book is dedicated to all of the African-American workers who currently serve their clients with these traditions. To the women who dared to not follow the rules; I stand in gratitude to you now and always. And, finally, this book is dedicated to Sojourner Truth: You may have died 95 years before I was born, but your story, your voice, and your spirit have guided me more than any living person possibly could. What is remembered lives.

ACKNOWLEDGEMENTS

Thanks to Catherine Yronwode, for your support, your wisdom, your willingness, and for all the chances you've taken on me over the years.

Thank you, Nagasiva Yronwode, for being one of the most patient and clear people I have ever met.

Thank you, Charles Porterfield, for your good advice, for all the laughs, and for your grounded strength.

Thank you, Greywolf Townsend, for making my books look beautiful.

Thanks to my colleagues who contributed: Aura Laforest, ConjureMan Ali, Lou Florez, Miss Michæle, Charles Porterfield, Madame Pamita, and Cat Yronwode — and to those who taught this work to Rev. Harry Hyatt.

I want to thank my husband and partner Gwion Raven and my daughter Trinity. Toward the end of this process, I was so focused on writing that I started dreaming about money spells. Interesting, indeed (!), but also all-consuming. Thank you both for your patience and understanding as I pulled it all together and worked more hours than I thought humanly possible.

And a big thank you to Lisa, Ariel, and Xenia, the beautiful Goddesses who kept my shop and business running while I centered my energy on this book. I would be lost without you all!

WHY THIS BOOK?

I am fascinated by people's relationships with money and success. For some folks wealth comes smoothly and easily and for others it is a struggle and a fight. I find it curious that financial gain, something that should be so simple, ties people in knots and leaves folks suffering. Not everyone is going to be rich, and hitting the multi-millions in the lottery is a long shot, but living under hand to mouth circumstances is totally changeable. The one thing I know about magic is you DO have the power to change your situation and improve your life. That's the whole point of being a hoodoo practitioner — to change our circumstances for the better.

I have a friend who says that money is the root of all evil. My response to him is, "Yeah, that's why you're always broke, because you believe that!"

Think about it for a minute. What is the dollar bill in your wallet really worth? Seriously, what's it really worth? I'm not talking about the assumption of value that we might give it. That dollar in your pocket is just a piece of paper; its "real" value is nothing, except for maybe the warmth it would bring if you burned it. What gives that dollar any value is our belief in it. The collective belief of the people in the United States, the collective belief of people in other countries — these beliefs are the powers that give value to the small pieces of paper that we call currency. Belief cannot be seen or touched or held; belief is nothing more than energy.

Therefore, money is nothing but energy, and energy can be manipulated, shifted, changed, and controlled.

The first step with money and success magic is to have a good and positive relationship with money. If you, like my friend, think money is the root of all evil, then you need to change that relationship. If you don't have a good relationship with money, you are literally pushing money and success away from yourself. Improve your relationship with money and you will start to see your financial life improve.

Of course there are spells and magical tools in hoodoo that you can use to help improve your financial life. But as with any type of magical work, you need to make sure that you are taking smart financial steps every day to help your financial life too. You can't expect to get a loan if you don't apply for one. You can't expect to win the lotto if you never play. Do the rootwork and then take the "real world" steps to complete the process.

I'm not rich. You might expect that someone writing a book about money spells would be. However, I am wealthy in ways that don't reflect a million dollars in my bank account. I am able to create my own schedule, I get to do work that I love, I am lacking in nothing. I have prosperity on so many levels, and I know that these things spill out and help others, which just increases my own prosperity. I do work and I work hard. I am an excellent manifestor. When money is needed, I make it happen. When I need an extra windfall, I make it happen. When a financial situation needs to improve, I make it happen. And that's how hoodoo can help you too.

I have learned, and I want you to learn, that money and success require reciprocal movement. When you have a success, that gift must move. You have to pay it forward. It is an old-school tradition that if a root doctor gives you a lucky number or sets a money light for you and you win big, you give a tip to your worker. You have to pay it forward; you need to share your success. There are also conjure spells that involve placing dressed money in the pages of a Bible, and after a time donating that money to charity. You do the work and you pay it forward. The gift must move.

Since the earliest times, humans have bartered and traded: "Hey, you've got some berries; would you give me some if I give you some roots?" Bartering and trading worked for a long time. But money, the symbolic representation of goods, has been around for almost as long. It's believed that as early as 5000 BCE people were using metal objects as a form of currency, and paper money has been traced back to 10th century China.

There are three ways to value money. First, there is its commodity value. If a coin is melted down, the metal has a real value. Second, there is its face value. When governments mint coins and certify their weight and content, they add a fee or tax, called "seigniorage," for their service. The face value of a coin is its commodity value plus the seigniorage that was charged. Finally, there is fiat money. This is "money because I say it is money." It is something essentially worthless that is decreed to have a value by the issuing body. Modern paper currency and base-metal coins are fiat money.

The disconnect from real world value to believed value is getting wider. Many people don't use cash anymore. Carrying personal checks is considered old-fashioned. Most of us have magical plastic cards that hold all of our financial worth on them. We borrow money or purchase goods with these plastic cards. Some of us have electronic accounts whereby we receive, transfer, or spend money by simply clicking keys on a keyboard.

The tangible nature of money as a commodity or coinage has faded away and what we are left with is belief — belief that money is important, that it has intrinsic value, that it is a real thing. This is actually good for us rootworkers. The movement of numbers from computer to computer is easier to influence than the coins or bills in someone else's pocket.

And let's be clear here: money is still, and always will be, a "real" thing. Even though you may rarely carry cash, even if you use a debit card or electronic fund transfers for all your purchases, money is still the way you measure value, and it will be for the foreseeable future. Getting in a right relationship with money will allow your finances to improve and invite more abundance and wealth to come your way.

I've often been asked, especially by "spiritual" folks, about the ethics of money magic. Remember my friend who thought that "money is the root of all evil"? He had the quote wrong, for in the Bible, at 1 Timothy 6:10, it is written that, *The love of money is the root of all evil."* That concept of an illicit "love" of money points to an underlying fear that the deadly sin of greed is inherent in money work, as if desiring to pay bills, have nice things, take care of your family, and live a comfortable life were greedy! But holding a desire for material goods does not make you a greedy person, and nice cars, big houses, or large bank accounts, are not signs of greed.

Greed is a problem because it never ends. Consuming just to consume or buying material goods because you think they will make you happy is an empty pursuit. If you are coming from a place of greed you will always find another thing to desire. Achieving your desires will not bring fulfillment, or if it does, your satiation will at best be temporary. Having less money does not put an end to greed, The only way to counteract greed is to find satisfaction. This is why I encourage my clients and students to really look at the items and the conditions they desire. Instead of chasing after things that will never bring satisfaction, allow yourself to look a little bit deeper.

What I find important in spell work around money is to look at the need underlying your initial desire. If you want to work a spell for more money, that's all fine and good, but what would "more money" actually create for you? Would more money bring peace of mind? Would more money bring security? Would more money bring happiness? What is your true need? That is where I encourage you to focus your energy.

Go after your goals, make big wishes, and call in your financial dreams!

— Phœnix LeFæ

ᴀN INTRODUCTION TO ᴴOODOO

Hoodoo is a compilation of folkloric medicinal remedies, folk magic, spirituality, spiritual counselling, and customs that developed in the African-American South, with deeper roots going back to the continent of Africa. It is known by many regional names, including conjure, throwing roots, rootwork, using that stuff, tricking, laying tricks, goofering, and jomo work. During the era of the Transatlantic slave trade, Africans from diverse tribes brought their magic with them, and once in America, they adapted it to the new continent and mingled their practices with Native American herbology, Jewish scriptural magic, and Christian European folklore.

After the Civil War, African-Americans moved beyond the borders of the South, reaching all across the United States. The 20th century brought increasingly open contact between Americans of varying cultures, along with a rapidly evolving series of technological advances that affected how everyone lived. Hoodoo changed with the times, and mail order catalogues made magical herbs, roots, curios, oils, candles, and books available to people for whom hoodoo was not their family's tradition. The technology of the 21st century has taken this even further, giving hoodoo a global access point on the internet. Now you will find practitioners all around the world, each one adding personal touches to the tapestry of conjure work.

Many hoodoo practitioners belong to Baptist or Spiritualist churches, but hoodoo itself is not a religion. There is no initiation into the mysteries of hoodoo. The Bible is an important magical tool in conjure, prayer is valuable, and understanding the "doctrine of signatures" is helpful, but none of these are required. You don't have to know a secret handshake, learn a password, or enter a special hoodoo temple to learn the work.

Hoodoo started as an oral tradition, with tricks, spells, and remedies being passed verbally from one family member to another. This is why we find many differing regional practices, recipes, and spells in the work. Just like folk songs, which have no "official" lyrics, folk magic incorporates a range of variations. Yet despite the variations, hoodoo is built upon shared foundational beliefs, and respecting them is vital. A good practitioner, regardless of ethnicity, understands these origins and honours the culture-bearers who transmitted the knowledge, and their descendants who still claim it. Acknowledging our debt to African-American culture is essential.

WHERE DO THESE SPELLS COME FROM?

Money magic can be found wherever money is found — but in rural communities, abundance comes from farming and hunting, and wealth is measured in terms of food stocks, not coins. In such places, spells are cast to make it rain, draw fish and game, and give power to tools and weapons. If you wish to study this type of magic, I recommend *"Trolldom: Spells and Methods of the Norse Folk Magic Tradition"* by Johannes Gardback. It contains 500 years of Scandinavian spells for fishing, hunting, and farming.

With increasing urbanization, the pastoral magic of abundance shifts to an emphasis on attracting and multiplying money. Professional root doctors adapt old spells and create new ones all the time, but the down-home methods and terms still remain, embedded in modern folk magic. For example, we speak of "trained hunting money," which reflects the training of hunting dogs. Likewise we work with living plants, and we ask that, "as this grows, so will my money grow," reflecting a farmer's hope for bountiful crops. We oil and dress our coins, and call them "seed money" in emulation of farming magic. In America, because our paper currency is the "greenback dollar," we treat it as a crop, and use the farmer's colour, green, to draw more money to us. We may even make "a little nest" of dollar bills and coins, on which we set a lodestone, resembling a Hen upon her eggs.

In honouring conjure's past, it is our good luck that much of this history has been preserved. Among the many people who collected and published African-American spells in the 20th century, let us tip our hats to:

- **Helen Pitkin:** The probable author of *Black and White Magic of Marie Laveau,* a collection of old New Orleans spells published in the 1920s.
- **Newbell Niles Puckett:** A White folklorist who interviewed 400 Black practitioners for *Folk Beliefs of the Southern Negro,* published in 1926.
- **Zora Neale Hurston:** An African-American folklorist whose book on hoodoo practices, *Mules and Men,* was published in 1935.
- **Harry M. Hyatt:** From 1936 to 1970, Rev. Hyatt interviewed 1,600 African-American practitioners in 13 states, collecting 13,400 spells in *Hoodoo - Conjuration - Witchcraft - Rootwork* (5 volumes, 1970 - 1978). We know some by name and others only by their Informant Number.

And so I bring you a mixed bouquet of magic; old, new, rural, and urban.

CONJURE TERMS AND TECHNIQUES

Here is a basic vocabulary of words and concepts found in hoodoo and other forms of folk magic. Books dedicated to these topics are noted as well.

- **Altar:** A surface set aside for spellcrafting, veneration, or devotion. See *"Hoodoo Shrines and Altars"* by Miss Phœnix LeFæ.
- **Anointing:** To dress with an oil in a reverential context; see Dressing.
- **Baths:** Water with herbs, salts, or oils; baths remove negativity or draw in desired conditions. See *"Hoodoo Spiritual Baths"* by Aura Laforest.
- **Bottle and Jar Spells:** Used to hold specific types of work; containers can be kept on altars, buried, floated away, shaken, or smashed.
- **Candle Work:** Spells centered on burning or manipulating candles. See *"The Art of Hoodoo Candle Magic"* by Catherine Yronwode.
- **Carrying, Toting:** Wearing a curio or mojo hidden on your person.
- **Chamber Lye:** A common, albeit old-fashioned, word for urine.
- **Cleansing:** The prescribed removal of spiritual dross or uncleanness.
- **Condition:** The circumstance that lead a person to work conjure.
- **Condition Oils, Incense, Sachets, Baths:** Spiritual supplies used to enhance, remedy, or prevent specific conditions.
- **Conjure:** An old English term for casting magic; see Rootwork.
- **Contact Magic:** A spell touched by the person you seek to affect.
- **Crossed Conditions:** Negative situations; often the result of a jinx or a crossing spell; less serious than a curse; remediated by uncrossing.
- **Curio:** A physical item used in rootwork, such as a root, coin, bone, stone, or amulet; it may be natural or manufactured.
- **Divination:** Spirit-led prophesy about people, places, or conditions.
- **Doll-Baby:** A magical effigy or poppet used as a stand-in for a person.
- **Dressing:** To rub an item with an oil; derived from dressing leather.
- **Fixing:** To prepare a magical item with herbs, oils, or curios.
- **Floor Wash:** Spiritual supplies used to clean a home or place of business. See *"Hoodoo Spiritual Baths"* by Aura Laforest.
- **Foot-Track Spell:** Sympathetic magic with a person's foot-track dirt.
- **Freezer Spell:** Sympathetic magic with ice or in a freezer to stop someone, slow something down, or freeze someone in their tracks.
- **Jinx:** A minor spell by which someone steals or cuts off your luck.

- **Herbs and Roots:** Plant matter used in spells and spiritual supplies. See *"Hoodoo Herb and Root Magic"* by Catherine Yronwode.
- **Honey or Sugar Spell:** Sweets are used to sweeten people. For more information see *"Hoodoo Honey and Sugar Spells"* by Deacon Millett.
- **Incense:** Smoke from fragrant smouldering plants used in rootwork.
- **Jack Ball:** A personal magical item to bring power and luck; hung by a string, it is also used for divination or to influence others.
- **Loading:** To fill a hole in a candle with curios, petitions, and personal concerns and to seal the hole with wax.
- **Mirror Spell:** Used to reverse evil spells back to the sender or to cause people to see themselves for who they really are.
- **Mojo Hand, Jomo, Toby, Nation Sack, Conjure Bag, Trick Bag:** A tied or sewn charm-bundle of herbs, roots, and curios. See *"The Art of Making Mojos"* by Catherine Yronwode.
- **Personal Concerns:** Hair, nails, skin cells, body fluids, handwriting, photographs, foot-track dirt, to help you connect to a person.
- **Petition:** The expression of a desired outcome.
- **Petition Paper:** A paper with a desire written on it. See *"Paper in My Shoe"* by Catherine Yronwode.
- **Psalms:** A book of the Bible containing many petitions and curses. See *"Hoodoo Bible Magic"* by Miss Michæle and Prof. C. D. Porterfield.
- **Prayer:** Praise or petitions directed toward a deity, angel, or spirit.
- **Reading:** Divination by visual cues like cards, bibliomancy, or wax.
- **Rootwork:** Another name for hoodoo; specifically plant-based.
- **Sachet Powders:** Scented powders that are sprinkled, laid down, blown about, hidden, used to dress papers, or dusted onto candles.
- **Setting Lights:** Altar work utilizing stationary lamps or candles.
- **Spiritual Supplies:** Manufactured goods used in the practice of magic.
- **Sympathetic Magic:** To use a stand-in item to connect to a person.
- **Trained Hunting Money:** Currency used to draw more money to you.
- **Trick, Tricking:** A regional term for hoodoo; a trick is a spell, a tricked item is a fixed item, and a trick bag is a mojo hand.
- **Uncrossing Spell:** A spell worked to take off a jinx or crossed conditions. See *"Deliverance!"* by Khi Armand.
- **Witchcraft:** An old English term for folk magic, it also became a regional term for African-American hoodoo or rootwork.
- **Work:** A euphemism for throwing roots, spells, conjure, or casting.

Doing Your Spells "Right"

HOW TO DEVELOP FOCUS AND FAITH

Conjure, like all other forms of folk magic, ceremonial ritual, and religious devotion, requires that you bring knowledge, active desire, will-power, focus, and faith to your work. Your will, your belief, and your spiritual concentration are essential. If you find yourself distracted, worried, shaken, fearful, or out of sorts while casting a spell, you may have difficulty performing the work in a smooth, orderly, and graceful manner, and this could create a weak outcome or undercut your success.

Concentration isn't always easy. It takes practice. You have to focus on what you are doing and trust in your skills and abilities. You will benefit from repetition: Setting your first light may seem strange, but after you have lit and prayed over a hundred, the work will be second nature to you.

Because money magic is generally uplifting and positive, faith is easy to maintain if you understand that, just as with mundane work like carpentry or cooking, not every spell invariably produces the exactly expected result. Magic involves the manipulation of subtle energies, so there are inherent subtleties in spell-casting outcomes. Sometimes the thing that you were working for comes in a slightly different way than you were expecting. Accept whatever abundance you are given and use it with confidence.

HOW TO STAY IN THE MOMENT

For some people, the greatest challenges to concentration come when deploying a trick or disposing of spell remains. The reason that these can be so difficult is that you may have to deal with or be seen by other people. You won't have the privacy or comfort of your own space. You may have to deal with strangers watching you, or asking what you are doing. Use such encounters as a way to develop your bravery and courage.

Another challenge is the doubt that undermines your faith. During the small moments, the quiet moments, self-doubts sneak in. While lighting a candle or setting out your supplies, you may notice a little voice in the back of your head that tries to shake your faith or your confidence. Your skeptical mind might start telling you that none of this is real. That voice might stop you cold by asking, "What the heck are you doing? This is a waste of time." That voice needs to be quieted. Thank it and dismiss it.

HOW TO RECOVER FROM LOSS OF CONCENTRATION

Picture this: You have all of your spell implements laid out. Your prayer is written. Your dressed and blessed coins are set in front of you, You open your mouth and take a breath to start the recitation of your Psalm — and the doorbell rings. It's your neighbour telling you that your Dog got out of the back gate. Now you have to go wrangle your pup, get her back in the house, and try to regain the sense of calm and focus you had before.

It might be difficult to just jump right back into the spell. You may find yourself frustrated with your Dog, concerned that there is a hole in the fence, grateful to your neighbour for letting you know what was going on. But none of these thoughts is connected to the rootwork at hand.

This is where you get to really attend to your spiritual practice. Don't become frustrated. Don't give up. Don't take it as a sign that your work is blocked or doomed. Here are a few proven ways to bring your focus back:

- **Pray:** Call on God, your spirit allies, or your ancestors. Ask them to help you get back into the calm place you need for your rootwork.
- **Recite:** If you know the Lord's Prayer or the 23rd Psalm by heart, recite it until you feel fully in your body, focussed on the work.
- **Breathe:** Allow yourself to breathe clearly and slowly until you feel yourself calm and focussed. Breathing in the scent of flowers also helps.
- **Spray:** Dissolve some Clarity Bath Crystals into a spray bottle and spray this above your head. Let this mixture bring you focus.
- **Cense:** Burn Clarity Incense or dried Sage and smoke yourself in it. Allow the smoke to call you back to yourself and to your focus.
- **Move Your Body:** Shake yourself, stretch your muscles, take a short walk, or do something else physical until you work off the distraction and move back into clarity.
- **Wash Up:** Wash your hands in the sink, and splash Florida Water in your palms. Rub your palms along the back of your neck, up onto your face, across your forehead, and then down your cheeks to your chin.
- **Do Something Else:** Wash the dishes, dust your living room, feed the Cat. Do something useful that is totally unrelated, to help to clear away the distraction so that you can come back refreshed.
- **Take a Break:** Set the work aside, walk away, and give yourself some time. If the energy is off, don't try to force it, just take a step back and return to your altar and your spell when you feel more grounded.

Traditional Money-Drawing Tricks

Following the instructions in a spell book as if it were a cookbook gives you a clear and direct plan, but you will have a better chance of success if you understand the methods that underlie the instructions. There isn't only one "right" way to do spells, but there are traditional ways to do them that have come down to us through a long line of practitioners who have done the work before us. Here are some tips and tricks used in money-drawing magic. They are not spells themselves, but rather ways to work your spells:

PRAYERS FOR PROSPERITY

When using Psalms in your conjure work, read or recite them out loud. Hear the words, focus on the prayer, and have faith. The following Bible Psalms have long been associated with money magic prayers:

- Psalms 4 (*"May it please Thee, O God to Prosper my ways..."*)
- Psalms 23 (*"The Lord is my shepherd, I shall not want ..."*)
- Psalms 61 (*"Hear my cry, O God; attend unto my prayer ..."*)
- Psalms 150, read three times (*"Praise ye the Lord ..."*)

For more information about scriptural magic for all conditions, see:
"Hoodoo Bible Magic" by Miss Michæle and Prof. C. D. Porterfield
For the full text and magical use of every Psalm, see this AIRR web page:
ReadersAndRootworkers.org/wiki/Category:The Book of Psalms

WORKING WITH SUGAR AND HONEY

Sweet spells are often associated with love magic, but they are just as effective when you want favours from someone in a position to hire you, raise your pay, loan you money, or offer you a discount on something you wish to purchase. Placing the person's name and photo in your sugar bowl and sweetening your morning coffee with the sugar is a classic trick.

For more on sweet spells, see this "Hoodoo in Theory and Practice" page:
LuckyMojo.com/honeyjar.html by Catherine Yronwode
For dozens of sweetening spells for use in all sorts of situations, read:
"Hoodoo Honey and Sugar Spells" by Deacon Millett

WORKING WITH HERBS, ROOTS, AND SPICES

Here are some of my favourite money-drawing botanicals:

- **Alfalfa:** For luck in gambling and business; to break money jinxes.
- **Alkanet:** This reddish-brown root bark protects your gambling wins.
- **Allspice:** Draws good luck and calms all anxious poverty-thoughts.
- **Bayberry:** For money drawing, used with candles or in a mojo.
- **Bergamot:** To influence others; to achieve goals despite competition.
- **Blue Flag:** Kept in your cash box so that your money never runs out.
- **Buckeye Nut:** A lucky pocket piece for gamblers and business people.
- **Calendula:** These golden flowers resemble coins; they draw in cash.
- **Cedar Wood:** To rent or buy real estate; to afford carpentry repairs.
- **Chamomile:** For winning games of chance; to clear off money jinxes.
- **Cinnamon:** For speedy and "hot" good luck in all money matters.
- **Cloves:** For friendship and for luck in friendly games of chance.
- **Comfrey Leaf or Root:** To keep your money safe while out and about.
- **Deer's Tongue:** For eloquent speech in loan-getting or in court.
- **Devil's Shoe Strings:** For money-luck at work or play; also protective.
- **Fenugreek Seed:** Related to Alfalfa; an ingredient in money mojos.
- **Five Finger Grass:** Its fingers help you grasp the money you need.
- **Grains of Paradise, Guinea Grains:** Hot and spicy for rapid luck.
- **High John the Conqueror:** For personal power, strength, and luck.
- **Irish Moss:** Dried seaweed; if carried, your money will never run out.
- **Little John to Chew:** For financial claims in court; to borrow money.
- **Lucky Hand Root:** Used to reach out and grab good luck and money.
- **Mace:** The covering of the Nutmeg; draws money in the sex trade.
- **Nutmeg:** For gambling luck; also used as a pendulum to pick numbers.
- **Patchouli:** Draws money, breaks jinxes, and clears financial blocks.
- **Rose of Jericho:** Kept alive in a place of business for growing wealth.
- **Sassafras:** Carried for success and steady increase in financial matters.
- **Thyme:** As it grows in your garden, so will your money increase.
- **Tobacco:** For financial luck, court cases, and influence over others.
- **Wintergreen:** For money drawing, especially if making a new start.
- **Yellow Dock:** The roots are boiled to make a business floor wash.

More information about botanical magic can be found in this book:
"Hoodoo Herb and Root Magic" by Catherine Yronwode

WORKING WITH SPIRITUAL SUPPLIES

Spiritual supplies combine herbs with other ingredients into magical products. Their names are generally secular, like Good Luck or Love Me.

- **Oils and Perfumes:** Wearing money oils and perfumes can set the stage for a job interview, a gambling adventure, or applying for a loan. Oils are also used to dress candles, to bless a business space, or used to anoint cash money, credit cards, amulets, or mojos.

For more on oils, see this Hoodoo in Theory and Practice web page: **LuckyMojo.com/oils.html by Catherine Yronwode**

- **Powders:** Sachet powders are dusted on the body, sprinkled in the shoes, and blown onto financial papers, including currency, invoices, purchase orders, and business cards. They can also be sprinkled under the mat in the entryway of a business to call in paying customers.

For more on powders, see this "Hoodoo in Theory and Practice" page: **LuckyMojo.com/powders.html by Catherine Yronwode**

- **Incense:** The fragrant scent of burning resins, herbs, and wood is a classic way to waft your prayers into the air. Smoke your cash in a money incense as you train it to collect more cash for you. Suffumigate yourself with gambling incense for better luck at the casino.

For more on incense, see this "Hoodoo in Theory and Practice" page: **LuckyMojo.com/incense.html by Catherine Yronwode**

- **Baths:** Bathing with money-luck spiritual supplies can help you to uncross or remove a money jinx. After the bad luck is washed away, a money-drawing bath can help you to call in the wealth and abundance you need. A gambling bath can help you to have better luck.

For more on baths, see this "Hoodoo in Theory and Practice" page: **LuckyMojo.com/baths.html by Catherine Yronwode**
For further information on baths, with spells and recipes, read:
"Hoodoo Spiritual Baths" by Aura Laforest

FAVOURITE FORMULAS FOR MONEY-LUCK

Although you may mix the herbs and roots listed on page 15 to make your own spiritual supplies, the commercial manufacture of such goods has been a part of hoodoo since around 1900. Each maker has his or her own recipes, but here are the best known formula-names in money magic:

- **Algiers:** A rapid-acting luck attractor, similar to Fast Luck.
- **Attraction:** To draw both money and love at the same time.
- **Aunt Sally's Lucky Dream:** To dream of lucky numbers for betting.
- **Black Cat:** When a situation is risky, this brings "reverse bad luck."
- **Boss Fix:** To get your boss to give you a raise or a promotion.
- **Crown of Success:** Add it to money formulas for career success.
- **Double Luck Perfume Oil:** A two-way blend for money and love.
- **Fast Luck:** For quick and lucky results in business or gambling.
- **Five Finger Grass:** For luck at games where the hands must be nimble.
- **Gambler's Gold Lucky Seven Hand Wash:** A lucky herbal wash.
- **Good Luck:** To draw love and money; for success in all aspects of life.
- **Hoyt's Cologne:** A perfume or aftershave to win in games of chance.
- **King Solomon Wisdom:** For wise and profitable business decisions.
- **Lady Luck:** The choice of many women who go to the casinos to play.
- **Lodestone:** To draw to you what you desire in money, luck, and love.
- **Lucky Buddha:** For monetary wealth with the Lucky Hotei Buddha.
- **Lucky Hand:** A popular hand dressing for dice and card players.
- **Lucky Mojo:** For horse races, lotto, sweepstakes, and games of chance.
- **Lucky Money Herb Mix (Besamim Spices):** For money and luck.
- **Lucky Number:** For numbers to bet from a dream or numerology.
- **Lucky 13:** For lottery play when there are long odds of winning.
- **Magnet:** To draw whatever you desire in luck, money, and love.
- **Money Drawing:** The classic, best-selling, and most-loved formula.
- **Money House Blessing:** Income for those who work from home.
- **Money Stay With Me:** It's not how much you get; it's what you keep.
- **Pay Me:** For the return of money owed; to secure a promised fee.
- **Prosperity:** To increase earnings, savings, and retirement funds.
- **Seven Herb Bath:** To draw luck in love, life, money, and games.
- **Steady Work:** To get and keep a good job; to avoid being laid off.
- **Three Jacks and a King:** To improve skill and luck at cards.
- **Wealthy Way:** To bring in cash for luxuries and status symbols.

WORKING WITH CANDLES

Since the mid-1930s, the use of candles has become an increasingly popular method of performing conjure spells of all kinds. A candle brings warmth, glow, and energy into its space. Even if not dressed or prayed over, when a candle is lit, it changes the atmosphere. There is something inherently special about the light of a candle, and candle spells are simple, easy, and adaptable to many conditions. This is why candle magic is often the first step that novice conjure doctors take as they learn to work in this tradition. In addition to moving your wishes toward manifestation, candles can also be used in divination, for the melted wax and smoke patterns will tell you if there is success or a road block up ahead.

Popular forms of candles are 4-inch, 6-inch, and 9-inch free-standing candles, glass-encased vigil lights, votives and tea lights, and symbolic or figural candles. Green, yellow, gold, or silver candles are typically used for money work, as these colours represent good crops, currency, and coins.

For further information on candle spells of every kind, see this book:
"The Art of Hoodoo Candle Magic" by Catherine Yronwode

WORKING WITH MOJO HANDS

A mojo, jomo, or conjure hand is a powerful living amulet, your ally in any type of work. At the most basic level it is a bundle of small curios wrapped, tied, or sewn in cloth or leather. Traditional mojos are often made in red flannel, but modern workers may use a range of symbolic colours.

When creating money mojos, I like to work with green fabric, and choose ingredients that have a specific alignment with prosperity — for example, Five Finger Grass, a Mercury dime, a lodestone, and a pinch of magnetic sand. I place them in a little green bag, dress and bless the bag, breathe life into it, pull and tie the string, smoke it in a money incense, give it a little drink of whiskey, and I've got a powerful mojo to help call in abundance.

Once you've given your mojo life, you must keep it hidden at all times. Never let anyone else see your mojo. Wear it on your body, or in your pocket. Keep it safe. Feed it whiskey, oil, spirits, or incense smoke often. You want your mojo to stay happy.

For further information on mojos bags, with recipes, read this book:
"The Art of Making Mojos" by Catherine Yronwode

WORKING WITH LUCKY AMULETS AND CHARMS

Like other forms of folk magic, hoodoo includes the use of small amulets, charms, and talismans to be carried on the person or worn as jewelry. Because conjure is African-American — with emphasis on the "American" — these lucky charms were adopted over the past 150 years by workers who mingled socially with Americans of European and Asian descent. There are hundreds of such amulets; here are a few used in money magic:

- **All-Seeing Eye:** This is an open eye surrounded by rays of light. On the reverse of the Great Seal of the United States and on the back of every American one dollar bill, it is depicted within a triangle atop an unfinished pyramid. Above is the motto "Annuit Cœptis" (*"Providence favours our undertakings"*) and beneath is the motto "Novus Ordo Seclorum" (*"A new order of the ages"*). Thus, the eye and pyramid represent optimistic faith that the Divine prospers our money drawing.
- **Dollar Sign and Money Bag:** The blatant symbolization of money magic in the form of gold jewelry shaped like a dollar sign or a money bag is a bit over-the-top for some practitioners, but others clearly enjoy flaunting their ambitions. A dollar-sign-shaped money clip or a small money bag charm sewn onto a mojo bag may be more subtle.
- **Horseshoe:** The use of horseshoes for luck and protection is found in cultures where Horses have been important in labour, transportation, sports, or racetrack betting. The placement of the horseshoe, either with the "U" up or the "U" down, differs from culture to culture. To some, the upward "U" allows the horseshoe to catch good luck for the bearer; to others, the downward "U" pours out safety and abundance.
- **Lucky Numbers:** Certain games have winning numbers, and amulets can show a win. Lucky 7, Lucky 13, 3-4, 7-11, 21, 3-6-9, and 4-11-44 all hold meaning for those whose money is acquired by gambling luck.
- **Trunk-Up Elephant:** According to Indian traditions, Elephants are road openers who remove obstacles. This is reflected in the Hindu god Ganesha, who has the head of an Elephant. The idea of the "lucky" Elephant arose during British rule in India; in the United States many believe that an Elephant must have its trunk up to be a good luck charm.

For more lucky charms, see this "Hoodoo in Theory and Practice" page:
LuckyMojo.com/gamblersluck.html by Catherine Yronwode

WORKING WITH NATURAL CURIOS

Unlike manufactured charms, which may be modelled after natural curios in reduced size or in durable materials, the lucky items in this list are the actual things — botanical, mineral, or zoological:

- **Alligator Foot:** To increase gambling luck, an Alligator foot may be worn as a key chain charm or carried in a mojo bag. This seems to be an American custom, for Alligators are indigenous to the Americas. The "clutching hand" of the foot also means that it can be used to hold folding money on an altar.
- **Buckeye Nut:** The Buckeye nut is often considered a lucky amulet for men, which brings virility and strength, but it is also connected to gambling luck. Anointed with Fast Luck Oil, it may be kept in the pocket for help when playing games of chance.
- **High John the Conqueror Root:** This hard, brown root is used for power, prosperity, and success. Zora Neale Hurston recorded that it is named after a rebellious slave who became an inspiration to others. As a "man's" curio, it is placed in mojo hands for male virility because it does resemble testicles, but truth to tell, women will tote a High John Root on them just as well, especially for money drawing and good luck.
- **Lodestone:** A form of iron ore, called magnetite, that holds a slight magnetic charge, it is employed to draw or call something toward you, such as money or a partner in love. Lodestones are fed by sprinkling them with magnetic sand or anvil dust. If they get dusty, wash them in whiskey, and dress them with a money oil. They have a natural affinity for coins and currency, and may be used together.
- **Lucky Stone, Fish Head Bone, Drumfish Otolith:** The ear bones of several species of fish — notably the Freshwater Drumfish or Croaker, the Drum Redfish or Puppy Drum, and the larger Catfish — are carried and kept in pairs for good luck in gambling, business, and money matters. Like the Raccoon penis bone, they entered hoodoo through contact with Native Americans, who consider them very lucky.
- **Nutmeg:** This fragrant spice has been a valued article of trade for hundreds of years. Because it keeps its scent best if stored in whole form, the Nutmeg, like the Buckeye and High John the Conqueror, is a symbol of health, strength, and money luck that is oiled and carried in a mojo, or kept in a pocket while playing games of chance.

- **Pyrite:** A non-magnetic iron ore, pyrite is also known as fool's gold because its yellow glint resembles gold. This stone may not have a large monetary value, but it does have a large magical value. A fist-sized piece goes on your altar. Small pieces go in mojo bags. When crushed to grit, it is used to dress vigil candles, sprinkle on a lodestone, dust into your wallet, or scatter on the change in your business cash register.
- **Rabbit Foot:** An old rural charm for hunting magic and good luck, it is carried on the person, often on a key chain. You can rub it to change bad luck to good. There are numerous regional beliefs about how to hunt the Rabbit, which foot is luckiest, and which colour fur is best; but, basically, the Rabbit foot brings money luck no matter how you use it.
- **Rattlesnake Rattle:** The Rattlesnake is a New World species and entered hoodoo through contact with Native American magic. It is a symbol of bravery *("Don't tread on me")* and of winning, especially in musical contests or at the gambling table. Musicians place a rattle in the body of a guitar or fiddle; gamblers keep one in a glass or metal tube.
- **Raccoon Penis Bone:** Mammalian penis bones are used in love spells or for sexual prowess. The Raccoon is an American species brought into hoodoo from Native American magic. In addition to its employment in spells of love and marital fidelity, the Raccoon penis bone, when wrapped with paper currency, is a good luck charm for gambling.
- **Rose of Jericho:** This North African plant shrivels to a ball during times of drought and looks dead. As soon as it gets wet it will reopen and turn green. It can stay dormant for years and still come back to life, which is why it is also called the Resurrection Plant. The Rose of Jericho is an excellent magical tool for keeping money.
- **Sand Dollar:** This is the shell of a flattened species of Sea Urchin. Too large and fragile to carry on the person, it makes a great altar piece. Fossilized Sand Dollars are equally popular on money altars.
- **Wishbone:** The furcula or fused clavicle bone of a bird, typically a Turkey or Chicken, is saved after the bird is cooked and allowed to dry until it is easy to snap. Two people each make a silent wish and pull the wishbone. Whoever ends up with the larger piece will have his or her wish granted. In America this rite is often associated with Thanksgiving.

Read more about good luck curios at the "Lucky W Amulet Archive" site:
LuckyMojo.com/luckyw.html by Catherine Yronwode

GETTING LUCKY NUMBERS FROM DREAM BOOKS

As Cat Yronwode explains: "Dream books are used to catch lucky numbers. They link dream images (e.g. dream of a cook or dream of a locomotive) to divinatory meanings (e.g. "you will receive a letter" or "beware a strange man") and they also give numbers for betting (e.g. 5-14-50 or 65-41-55). In a typical numbers book, the dream images are listed in alphabetical order, with one, two, three, or four numbers beside each item." Using a dream book to catch lucky numbers for lottery play is an old time gambler's trick, and one that is still used by many a lottery winner.

Learn the use of dream books in "Hoodoo in Theory and Practice" online: **LuckyMojo.com/auntsallys.html by Catherine Yronwode**

USING MONEY TO DRAW MONEY

Cash money is a powerful ally when it comes to money magic. You can train your cash (or even your credit cards) to do the work on your behalf. This is ongoing, continuous, and simple work found in many spells.

Currency spells begin with a paper bill. Use the largest denomination that you have. For me this is often a ten or a twenty, but fifty or one hundred dollar bills are even better. Sign your name right on top of the signature of the Secretary of Treasury and set it in a safe place. Every week (or every day, if you can afford it) prepare another bill. This currency will be used in a variety of spells, some for drawing money and some for retaining or accumulating it.

Coin spells are similar. You start with a few coins and a bowl to keep them in. The number of coins to add each day is an individual preference, and can range from "all my pennies" or "all my quarters" to "one coin of each denomination every day." Some folks only put "special" coins aside, such as those with dates that are significant to them, images they like, or images that represent the financial goal toward which they are working. For instance, National Park Quarters are great for vacation plans, State Quarters may help in moving to a new state, and Sacagawea dollar coins are a natural image to signify a working mom who wants to start her own home business or get back in the job market. Whatever coins you choose, dress each one with oil as you put it in your bowl. Spells in which these coins are used include those for money blessing, money drawing, business building, money keeping, gambling, and the accumulation of wealth.

WORKING WITH RARE COINS AND BILLS

Using rare coins in your rootwork adds a boost to your spells. A rare bill or coin is worth more than its face value. It is already a money spell, just by its very existence. If a penny is actually worth $50.00 that's some pretty effective magic! You don't need to be a money collector to work with rare coins, bills, and currency. There are lots of rare pieces out there; you might have one in your pocket right now and not even know it. Here are some rare coins and currency that are possible to find, and great for money spells.

- **Indian Head Cents:** These lucky and protective "Scout" coins are rarely found in circulation anymore, as they were minted from 1864 to 1909, but they can be had at most coin shops for a few dollars each.
- **Wheat Pennies:** Made from 1909 to 1958, these have Lincoln on the front and wheat sheaves on the back. Rarities like the 1909-S VDB, are worth thousands, but most can be had for few cents to a few bucks.
- **Mercury Dimes:** Winged Liberty or so-called "Mercury" dimes were minted from 1916 to 1945. They are worth more than a dollar because of their high silver content. Finding a Mercury dime is a sign of good luck, and they are traditionally used for money drawing and protection.
- **1972 Double-Die Lincoln Cent:** This coin had a minting flaw that resulted in all of the letters on the front being double-printed. It can be missed at first glance, but look closely — it's worth $500.00 or more.
- **1982-No-P Dime:** Due to a minting error, the letter "P" (for "Philadelphia") that should have been stamped right above the year is missing. As a result, this ten cent coin is worth $30.00 to $50.00.
- **2004-D Wisconsin State Quarter:** Due to a flaw in the die, some Wisconsin state quarters minted in Denver have an extra leaf in the ear of corn. This coin is still in circulation and worth $100.00 to $200.00.
- **Two Dollar Bills:** Although a two dollar bill is rare, they are still in circulation. You can get a two dollar bill at any bank with no problem. They aren't printed as often as other bills, but they are still legal tender.

For more information on lucky money, see these "Lucky W" web pages:
LuckyMojo.com/goodluckcoins.html by Catherine Yronwode
LuckyMojo.com/silverdime.html by Catherine Yronwode
For instructions on divination with State Quarters, see this book:
"Lithomancy" by Jon Saint Germain

WORKING WITH CHINESE SPIRIT MONEY

The African roots of hoodoo developed in cultures with strong religious traditions of ancestor veneration. Petitioning the ancestors to help the living is one of many ways of changing luck and getting good fortune. When your ancestors are working on your behalf you have a better chance of success.

The Chinese concept of ancestor veneration is just as strong, in its own way, as the African beliefs. The two cultures have, on the face of it, little in common, but both pay great honour and respect to the familial dead. Had people of African and Chinese descent never met, nothing would have come of it, but in America, they did meet and the result was amazing.

The phrase "Hell Money" might sound negative, but it actually doesn't hold that connotation. When Christian missionaries arrived in China, they told Taoists and Animists that they would "go to Hell" when they died. The Chinese thus understood "Hell" as the realm of the ancestors. Chinese culture is deeply imbued with ancestor veneration. Paper offerings are regularly burned for the beloved dead to bring them the good things they enjoyed in life. Hell Bank Notes are monetary offerings or spirit money for the ancestors. Printed in bright colours, they look like decorative currency, and they feature a central image of the Emperor of the Afterworld.

Spirit money entered conjure long ago as a way to work with and pay our ancestors, give them offerings, and ask them for financial help. Hell Notes are also used as petition papers in money spells or as decorations for money altars. They can be added to mojo bags or given as payment to crossroads spirits or graveyard spirits who are paid for their assistance.

There are, of course, some root doctors who say that Chinese spirit money is inauthentic because only "real money" can be given to ancestors. Their doctrinal rigidity, however, fails to address the generations of African-American workers who happily lived among Chinese-American neighbours and adapted Hell Money (and Chinese joss stick incense) to their own uses. Regionality is always a factor in folk magic, and this is one instance where it can clearly be seen: A Black worker from San Francisco, New York, or Chicago may be familiar with, and may have used, Chinese goods, but to a worker from Little Rock, Arkansas, they might be unknown. Ask for Hell Bank Notes at your local Chinese market — or find them online.

See samples of Chinese spirit money and read more on this web page: **LuckyMojo.com/hellmoney.html by Catherine Yronwode**

WORKING WITH THE STARS

Western astrology originated in the Middle East and spread to Europe and the Americas. By the mid-1920s, Black root doctors were regularly combining star magic with hoodoo. You don't have to be an astrologer to use zodiacal lore in your favour — just hire one! Once you have your natal horoscope, you can purchase yearly forecasts about your money luck.

- **Venus:** Known as the planet of love and beauty, Venus is also the planet of attraction, and as such it is connected to money and material things. With the energy of Venus you can call to you what you desire.
- **Jupiter:** The most important planet when it comes to success and prosperity, Jupiter symbolizes power, wealth, generosity, and wisdom. The energy of Jupiter can teach us about higher goals and philanthropy.
- **Second House:** The second house on your natal horoscope is your house of finances. This house will indicate how you connect to money matters and give you clues to income, wealth, and all financial issues.
- **Tenth House:** The tenth house is the house of career and vocation. The sign of this house on your natal chart will give you information on what you should be doing in the world to build fame and influence.
- **Moon Phases and Signs:** The waxing Moon is the best phase for money magic. Taking a cue from farmers' lore, start money growing when the Moon is in the fertile signs of Cancer, Pisces, and Scorpio.
- **Moon Void of Course:** As the Moon nears the end of its trip through each sign, it runs out of planets to aspect without changing signs and is Void of Course. Spells performed during this time generally fail.
- **Retrogrades:** When a planet is retrograde it can cause difficulties, delays, or mistakes. Knowing where the career or financial planets are on your natal chart will help you navigate periodic retrogrades.
- **Days of the Week:** Each day of the week is ruled by a planet, and some days are better for prosperity than others. Sunday, Thursday, Friday, and Monday are good, but avoid Saturday, the day of loss.
- **Astral Candle:** This is a free-standing candle in a colour suitable to your Sun sign, dipped halfway up in a second colour of wax to symbolize your rising sign. Corresponding herbs may be added as well.

Read more about astrology in "Hoodoo in Theory and Practice" online: **LuckyMojo.com/zodiacal.html by Catherine Yronwode**

DRESS AND BLESS FOR WEALTH AND SUCCESS

Dressing typically refers to the hand-application of a condition oil to a surface, but in casual usage, it can also mean blowing or dusting powders onto an object, or spraying it with an alcohol-based cologne or perfume. Any of the popular spiritual supply oils for money, gambling luck, and wealth that are listed on page 17 may be used, as well as whiskey, Hoyt's Cologne, or an oil-and-alcohol blend, like Double Luck Perfume.

Blessings are the prayers you make for your success. They can be simple petitions, such as, *"Lord, bless my hands in this endeavour,"* or scriptural recitations, such as the text of Psalms 23 *("The Lord is my shepherd...")*

Dressing and blessing are often done in tandem. The blessing is spoken aloud while the object is being dressed.

You are probably familiar with the practice of dressing and blessing yourself and your family, as well as the corners, doorways, and windows of your home or workplace and the items you use in your altar work, such as candles, incense braziers, divination tools, and statuary — but here are some other things to dress and bless for money, luck, and financial stability:

- Dress and bless the physical coins and paper currency you spend.
- Anoint your wallet as a money magnet to call more cash toward you.
- Dress your money clip or change purse for increased wealth.
- Bless your purse or wallet for money to stay with you and not be spent.
- Dress your credit cards to help you curb unnecessary spending.
- Dress and bless any gift cards that may be given to you.
- Keep your change in a piggy bank, dress the jar, and donate to charity.
- Dress and bless your safety deposit box; no one at the bank will know.
- Dust and bless any contracts or financial papers before signing them.
- Dust and bless the business cards you'll offer to prospective customers.
- Bless the change rolls from the bank before putting them in your till.
- Anoint a tip jar to help bring in bigger tips and loose change.
- Anoint altar lodestones to feed them with money-drawing energy.
- Anoint your shoes with oils or powders so every step leads to wealth.
- Dress your work tools: car, computer, hammer, briefcase, or uniform.
- Add money-drawing oils to your shampoo, conditioner, or body wash.
- Add money-drawing bath crystals to your washing machine loads.
- Anoint door handles at your job site to gain influence over co-workers.
- Sprinkle money powders at your business before you vacuum or sweep.

Money Drawing Goods offered by mail, 1895 - 2018. Art by Charles C. Dawson, Charles M. Quinlan, J. C. Strong, Grey Townsend, and Unknown Artists for Oracle Products, Famous Products, Standard O & B Supply, J. C. Strong, Indio Products, Eagle Supply, and the Lucky Mojo Curio Company.

Spells to Remove Money Blockages

If your money was obtained through sharp dealing, if you inherited cash that came from the streets, or if you damaged the livelihood of an innocent colleague, your money may be tainted. Alternatively, your finances may be blocked because a competitor has cursed your cash. These spells can help.

HYSSOP AND PRAYERS TO CLEANSE TAINTED MONEY

The Bible tells us in Psalms 51 how to take off a money taint: *"Purge me with Hyssop; wash me and I shall be whiter than snow."* Brew Hyssop tea, pray Psalms 51 over it, drink a cup of the tea, and use the rest to wash your body. To clean a location where financial improprieties took place, add Hyssop tea to Chinese Wash scrub water. Wash tainted coins in Hyssop tea.

UNCROSSING TAINTED CURRENCY IN YOUR WALLET

In *"Deliverance!"* Khi Armand writes: "An old-fashioned way to cleanse paper money is to put it in your wallet with dried whole Mint leaves. Write out Deuteronomy 8:18 *("Remember the Lord thy God: for it is he that giveth thee power to get wealth")* on one of the bills, and give that one to a beggar.

VAN VAN AND CHINESE WASH TO KILL A MONEY JINX

To clean off a money mess, prepare a bucket of scrub water with Chinese Wash and Van Van Oil, pray Psalms 23 *("The Lord is my shepherd ...")* and clean the premises top-to-bottom and back-to-front. Dispose of the dirty water off your property. If you get only partial relief, repeat the process a week later, adding Jinx Killer Oil to the Van Van and Chinese Wash. If you need a third go-round, wait a week and also add Uncrossing Oil to the mix.

DOUBLE ACTION CANDLE TO REVERSE A MONEY CURSE

Cut the green tip off a black-and-green double action candle and carve a new tip on the black end. This is called butting the light. It allows you to burn the candle upside-down, forcing the black curse to burn away, and leaving the green money to bless you. Carve your enemy's name backwards in the black half and your own name normally in the green half. Dress the black end with Reversing Oil and the green end with Money Drawing Oil. Set your candle stand on a mirror, praying to reverse the curse to the one who sent it.

CANDLE SPELL TO PROSPER AFTER AN ENEMY ATTACK

"The Master Book of Candle Burning" by Henri Gamache was among the first texts on African-American candle magic. In print since 1942, it describes the methods we now know as "moving candle spells," in which the candles enact conditions by proxy. This 7-day spell is an adaptation of Gamache's "Exercise No. 9: To Gain Prosperity." The original title gives no clue as to what the work is really about, but if you read the prescribed Biblical passage, you will soon understand that this is a spell to overcome a financial curse and all the social difficulties caused by a turncoat friend.

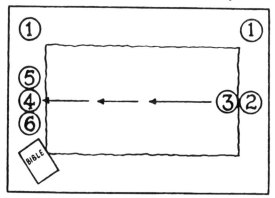

Positions 1 - 1: White Crucifix candles dressed with Holy Oil.

Position 2: Green candle with Prosperity and Crown of Success Oils.

Position 3: Yellow candle dressed with Attraction Oil.

Position 4: Your astral candle dressed with Zodiac Oil.

Position 5: Purple candle with John the Conqueror and Attraction Oils.

Position 6: Orange candle with Crucible of Courage and Attraction Oils.

Except for the crucifix candles, all the rest are 6-inch household candles in metal holders. The astral candle is of a colour suitable to your zodiac sign, dipped half-way up in wax whose colour is appropriate to your rising sign.

The Bible is kept open to Psalms 41 *("Blessed is he that considereth the poor ...")*. Read this aloud, light the candles, and burn them for 15 minutes. Candles 2 and 3 move two inches in the direction of the arrows each day.

According to Catherine Yronwode's original research, Henri Gamache was the pen-name of Anne Fleitman. Read more on this web page:

LuckyMojo.com/young.html by Catherine Yronwode

Spells to Bless Your Money

Blessing your money is much like blessing yourself, and many of the ways you might bless your body can be used to bless your cash, credit cards, and checks. Work with all forms of money, but be logical: While you and your coins can take a bath, your paper money can't, so it must be dusted or smoked — and don't put lodestones or magnets on your credit cards.

BLESSING YOUR CASH AND CREDIT CARDS

Dress a small green candle with Van Van Oil and light it. Empty your pockets of cash and coin. Clean out all of the money from your purse or wallet. Gather any coins that might be hiding in the couch cushions or the laundry. Add in your credit and debit cards. Set all of these things around the burning candle. Pray the 23rd Psalm over your pile of money and the candle. Dust the money with Blessing Sachet Powder. When the candle has finished, put your credit cards in a place that will require you to think before using them and put the coins and cash back in your wallet, purse, or pockets. Spend this blessed money with care and intention, knowing that for every penny that leaves your hand, more will return.

BLESSING "FOUND" COINS FOR LUCKY SPELL WORK

Coins found in the street are lucky, but they may need spiritual cleaning. Set them in a bowl, cover them with Florida Water, and pray Psalms 145:16 (*"Thou openest thine hand, and satisfiest the desire of every living thing."*) Voila, they are now ready to be used as good luck charms and altar items!

AURA LAFOREST'S COIN WASH BLESSING FOR THE POOR

Collect a double handful of brand-new coins in assorted denominations. Prepare a bath-tea with equal parts whole Cloves, Allspice berries, and Blue Flag root, plus a drop of honey. Strain the tea into a wash basin and "wash" each coin between your hands as you pray Psalms 23. Let the coins dry on a clean white cloth. When you go out in the streets, distribute the coins to the poor, for as it says in Deuteronomy 15:7: *"If there be among you a poor man of one of thy brethren within any of thy gates in thy land which the Lord thy God giveth thee, thou shalt not harden thine heart, nor shut thine hand from thy poor brother."* For this good deed you will be blessed.

Spells to Open Your Money Roads

If you have cleansed and blessed your money, but are still struggling to get employment or bring in cash, you might need a road opening.

AN EGG CLEANSING TO OPEN THE WAY

Begin by cleansing a raw egg with the Florida Water. Use just a little sprinkle to wash off the egg and then allow it to air dry.

Hold the egg in your hand and tell it that you want it to absorb any negativity of your body or mind, so that your roads may be open.

Roll the egg down the front of your body four times, from the top of your head to your feet, including the inner side and front of each arm and leg. Then roll the egg down the back side of your body four times, including the back and outer side of each arm and leg. If you need another person to help you, that is okay. If you drop the egg or it breaks, clean up and start over again. When you are done, carefully set the egg aside for a moment.

Splash a bit of Florida Water in your hands and wipe the back of your neck. Put a pinch of salt under your tongue. Anoint your feet, hands, knees, chest, forehead, and the top of your head with Road Opener Oil.

Now take the egg to a river of running water and throw it in, hard.

If you do not feel immediate results, repeat this process for three days.

FOUR ORANGE VIGIL LIGHTS TO OPEN YOUR ROADS

For this job you will need four glass-encased orange vigil candles. If they are plain and unlabelled, dress and bless them with Road Opener Oil and Road Opener Incense. If you prefer, you may purchase them pre-dressed and labelled as Road Opener Candles.

On a small piece of paper, write your petition: *"May all my roads be open for my financial success."* Place a pinch of Road Opener Sachet Powder in the center of the paper. Dust your altar space with Road Opener Sachet Powder in the form of an equal-armed cross (a crossroads) and put the paper in the center. Set the candles around your petition, on the paths of the crossroads. State your petition out loud three times and recite Psalms 23 as you light the candles. Each day as the candles burn, move them away from the center, down the "roads," to light and open your way. When the candles finish, wear the paper in your shoe as you walk your opened roads.

A PERSONAL ROAD OPENING VIGIL LIGHT

Print out your photo, and on the back write your name and birthdate. Print two images of horseshoes. Glue these images on a glass-encased orange candle. Be creative! Use Sharpie pens to draw open roads and the success sigil ($$¢¢$$) on the glass. Dress the candle with Road Opener Oil, Lemon Grass, and Road Opener Incense. Add copper glitter and gold stars.

On the back of a Joker from a deck of playing cards, write, *"May all my roads to successful and gainful employment be open and clear."* Set the candle on top of the card. Burn Road Opener Incense, light your candle, and state your wish. Burn the candle in sections or until it is finished, as you prefer. When the candle goes out, place a pinch of Lemon Grass in the center of the card, on the side with your petition. Fold the card three times, and tie it up with green thread or string to make a small, compact packet.

Keep the packet until you need it. Then dress the soles of your shoes with Road Opener Oil, carry the packet in your pocket, and know that you are clearing your way with every step that you take.

RECLAIMING ROADBLOCK SALT IN YOUR CORNERS

In *"Destroying Relationships"* by Miss Aida, you can read how people block a family's luck by leaving piles of salt in the corners of their homes. Here's how to turn that trick, as told to Rev. Hyatt in 1937 by Informant #556, a worker in Jacksonville, Florida: "Your enemies can bring salt from their home and put it into your place, cooking salt, see. Salt can be bad luck or good luck. And the same salt that they would give you hard luck with is also a means of good luck, in the four corners. If you find salt in your corners, or if you put down salt, you name each pile the kind of luck that you'd like to run in. For instance, you'd like to have this as the 'Money' pile; this other is some 'Prosperity,' this one is 'Love,' and this is 'Bigger Business.'"

SEVEN DAY ROAD OPENER MONEY CANDLE SPELL

Get seven 4-inch green candles, a candle holder, Road Opener Oil, and a Bible. Write your petition and lay it under the candle holder. Inscribe your name in the first candle, dress it with Road Opener Oil, open your Bible to Psalms 70 (*"Make haste, O God, to deliver me ..."*), and leave it open for all seven days. Pray the Psalm as you light one candle every night. On the last night close the Bible. If you are a Catholic, add a Saint Peter holy card to the petition, and lay a pair of crossed keys across the pages of the Bible.

SPELLS OF THE SEASON FOR WEALTH

There are certain times of the year where money magic is woven into the fabric of our traditions. One of these times is New Year's Eve.

MISS AIDA'S NEW YEAR'S EVE MONEY BATH
"Have on hand as many nickels, dimes, quarters, half dollar, and dollar coins as possible, I usually get rolls of them from the bank. Cleanse them before casting this spell. On New Year's Eve, at 11:40 PM, fill a bathtub with warm water and Money Drawing Bath Crystals. Put the coins in the tub. Between 11:50 and 11:55, sit in the tub. As 12:00 midnight approaches, start covering yourself with the coins. Pray Psalms 23, then say, *"I will be covered in money for the entire New Year."* Do not leave the bathtub until 12:05 AM or after. Dry the coins, dress a photo of yourself with Money Drawing Oil, put it in a container and cover it with the coins.

RECIPE FOR NEW YEAR'S HOPPIN' JOHN
There are many recipes for Hoppin' John, but no matter how you cook them, Black-Eyed Peas bring in money-luck for the year to come. This recipe comes to us courtesy of Calinda Bailey, in *"Hoodoo Food!"*

2 cups mixed black-eyed peas and kidney beans (luck)
3 quarts boiling water (cleansing and blessing)
¼ lb. bacon, diced (luck)
2 cups rice (prosperity and fertility)
¼ lb. spicy sausage, cubed (luck)
1 red onion, diced coarsely (luck)
Salt, black pepper, and red pepper to taste (protection)

Pour boiling water over beans and peas and let sit 1 hour. Add rice and cook on low heat until the beans are falling apart. Fry bacon and sausage; add onion and cook until golden; pour into beans and peas. Add spices to taste. Immediately after midnight, open every window and door in the house to let out any leftover bad luck. As soon as a particularly lucky person, such as a tall, strong man, walks in to set the tone of the luck for the New Year, serve the Hoppin' John with cornbread and honey.

Spells for Money Drawing

These spells will help you call in more abundance, more wealth, more prosperity, and just simply more cash for any purpose or need.

SEVEN COINS OF THE WAXING MOON BRING MONEY

This one-week spell is worked while the Moon is waxing and ends at the full Moon, to make your money grow. You will need seven 4-inch green chime candles and seven of the brassy metal "star-holders" they fit into. You will also need Money Drawing Oil, Good Luck Oil, and seven coins in increasing denominations. A cent, a nickel, a dime, a quarter, a half-dollar, and a dollar make six coins, so the seventh one will be your choice. For example, it can be a foreign nation's coin if you want to travel, a good luck token for general success, a poker chip if you like to play at the casinos, an angel token for blessings, or a 12-step sobriety medallion to symbolize your commitment to recovery.

Place the seven coins in a circle, and set a star-holder on each coin. Inscribe the seven candles with a simple money-wish. Dress them with Good Luck Oil and Money Drawing Oil, then roll them in powdered Cinnamon, Allspice, and Cloves (or pumpkin pie spices). If you'd like to, you can also add green or gold glitter to the spice powders. Set one candle in each holder. You will light one candle per evening just at sunset, moving around the circle in a clockwise manner. On the first night, light the first candle while reciting Psalms 23. It will burn for less than two hours. Leave the burned out candle in place, Each night light the next candle around the circle and recite Psalms 23. On the last night, the full Moon will be rising at sunset, while your last candle burns. When it goes out, the full Moon will be riding in the sky, as you collect your seven coins and put them in a little bag to carry for money growth.

SEVEN PENNY NECKLACE FOR MONEY

In April 1939, while stopping at the home of Henry L. Timmons, a taxi driver in Florence, South Carolina, Rev. Harry Hyatt interviewed Informant #1306, who shared a number of brief spells. Among other things, he said, "Wearing seven pennies 'round your neck; that's good luck to bring folks money. You can take and bore a hole — drill a hole in them."

THE SUCCESS SIGIL OR "MARKED MONEY"

This spell comes from *"Paper in My Shoe"* by Cat Yronwode:

"This was taught to me in the 1960s by the owner of a spiritual supply store in Oakland, California. All you need is a ballpoint pen and Money Drawing Sachet Powder or Money Drawing Oil or Hoyt's Cologne. In a pinch you can use whiskey instead of the oil or cologne.

"The 'SUCCESS sigil' is a special, cryptic way of writing the word 'success.' Try it out on paper before you do it on your money. Write:

SUCCESS

"Then write it again without the vowels, because we are only going to work with the consonants:

SCCSS

"Add an S to the front of the word so that the whole thing is a symmetrical palindrome (reading the same from front to back and back to front):

SSCCSS

"Then draw a line through each S to change it to a dollar sign $ and draw a line through each C to change it to a cent sign ¢:

$$¢¢$$

"That is the SUCCESS sigil — $$¢¢$$.

"Now that you know how to do it, take out every bill in your wallet. Write the $$¢¢$$ sigil diagonally in every corner of each of the bills. Underneath the name of the US Treasurer, write your own full name.

"Sprinkle the bills with Money Drawing Sachet Powder and drag your fingernails down them in 'wavy snake lines,' then shake the powder off. Dress the corners of each bill with a drop of Money Drawing Oil, Hoyt's Cologne, or whiskey as you say the 23rd Psalm (*'The Lord is my shepherd, i shall not want...'*). Put the dressed money back in your wallet.

"You can also write the $$¢¢$$ sigil in the form of a cross and use five of these crosses on a money-drawing petition, as Henry Buchy, a graduate of my Hoodoo Rootwork Correspondence Course, did above. His text is *'Bring Money Every Day / Bring Money in Every Way.'*"

TRAINING HUNTING MONEY WITH A LODESTONE

Lodestones are used to train money to hunt. The longer your cash is exposed to a money lodestone, the better a hunter it will be.

Create a small space on a window ledge, a book shelf, or the corner of a table or nightstand on which you will make a symbolic bird's nest, with currency as hay and coins as eggs. Set out a shallow bowl, place bills under it, and line the bottom with coins. If your bowl is wide enough, lay the currency in it and set the coins on top. Or, if you have a cash register, fold the currency to make the nest in one of the coin-holder sections.

Wash a large lodestone in whiskey, let it dry, and dress it with Money Drawing Oil. As you do this, listen to hear if your lodestone reveals its name to you. Not all stones have names and you may not be able to hear your stone, so if no name comes to you, then select a name for it, as you would for a pet. Because it is a living being, your lodestone will need regular feeding with magnetic sand or anvil dust, plus an occasional drop of whiskey or Money Drawing Oil. Speak to it as you feed it, and encourage it to impart its magnetism and drawing power to the money it is training.

Daily, or once a week, add new currency and coins under the lodestone. As the nest fills, start spending the money, using the older cash first, and continuing to replenish the nest with new bills and coins. As you spend the trained money, know that it is working to bring more cash to your pockets.

KHI ARMAND'S LUCKY COIN FROM AN ANCESTRAL LAND

"If your ancestors came to America under duress and the family is now poor, acquire an antique coin from the ancestral land as a token of 'what once was and may yet be.' Carry it as a prosperity talisman to enlist ancestral aid in regaining the family's wealth and status that was lost in the diaspora."

CUSTOM-MADE MONEY OIL AND A GREEN CANDLE

Blend John the Conqueror Oil, Bayberry Oil, and Cinnamon Oil into an Olive Oil base. Add a pinch of magnetic sand, pray over it, breathe life into it, and let it sit in a cool, dry place for seven days. Under the full Moon, carve money symbols and your name into a green candle, dress it with your oil, and put it in a candle holder that has a hollow in the bottom. Write a money petition, place a pinch of magnetic sand in the center of the paper, and fold, crumple, or twist it so that it will fit in the hollow of the candle holder. State your wish, light the candle, and let it burn down completely.

SAINT EXPEDITE CANDLE FOR QUICK MONEY

Saint Expedite is the patron saint for those who need rapid help, especially when it comes to financial needs. Many saints like offerings, but although it is traditional to give Saint Expedite offerings like pound cake, flowers (especially red Roses), coffee, or a glass of water, his offerings are always withheld until he comes through. That is, the offerings are only set out if he brings you money — but if he does come through and you fail to pay him, he is known to bring chaos or even death to your house. Start on a Wednesday, with a red glass-encased candle. Place a statue or print of Saint Expedite next to it and pray, *"Saint Expedite, I come to you and ask this wish be granted."* Name exactly the amount you need and exactly when you need it. Continue, *"Saint Expedite, I ask this wish be granted now. Do not delay! In faith, I know that you can help me. I will share your name with respect. I will bring you the gifts of pound cake and Roses. In the Lord's name, Amen."* Allow the candle to burn completely. If your wish is granted, fill the candle-glass with water, place red Roses in the glass, and set a piece of pound cake on a plate before the image.

BOILING SPICES FOR EMERGENCY NEEDS

When you need money for an emergency you don't always have the time to gather the perfect ingredients, so work with what you've got. On your stove boil water to which you have added common grocery store spices like Cinnamon, Allspice, Cloves, Nutmeg, Mace, or pumpkin pie spices, plus a pinch of sugar. Pray over this mixture as it boils. Write out your petition for exactly what you need and exactly when you need it. Fold the petition paper towards you, turn it clockwise, fold it again, and then repeat the pattern one more time. Soak the paper in the mixture and turn the heat back on. You may need to add water as it boils, but when your petition begins to dissolve, pour the mixture right outside your front door.

QUICK MONEY CALL CANDLE

Dress a small green candle with Fast Luck Oil and dust it with powdered Cinnamon. Carve symbols of money and income into the candle along with the dollar amount that you need. Place the candle in the center of four bright, clean pennies that have been dressed with Money Drawing Oil. When the candle has finished burning, take the pennies to the four corners of your town and leave them.

WALKING IN ABUNDANCE WITH BLACK SNAKE ROOT

Boil the largest Black Snake Root you can find in water for fifteen minutes. As the water boils, state your desire to walk in abundance. When the water is cool, strain it. Fill a glass bottle half way with vodka and add the Black Snake Root water. The vodka will act as a preservative. Every morning for seven days, shake the mixture, stating your desire as you shake. After the seventh day, dress your shoes with the water every morning. This way you will be walking in the Abundance Water that you have made.

MONEY DRAWING LAMP

Lamps are popular for ongoing rootwork, and when it comes to money drawing, it helps to shine your light so the money finds its way to you. You will need a glass kerosene oil lamp, purchased new at a hardware store or used at a thrift shop or online. You can buy oil for your lamp online or at a hardware store. Lamp oil comes in different colours, and you can choose between undyed or green oil for money. Place a Mercury dime, a pyrite chunk, pyrite grit, a lodestone, Magnetic Sand, a few drops of Patchouli oil, and a Cinnamon stick in the glass reservoir of your oil lamp. As you put each item in, speak your desire, petition, or prayer out loud. Write out your petition and place it under the glass base of the lamp. This petition can be rewritten and traded out as your financial needs change. Fill the reservoir with lamp oil, screw the burner on top, trim the wick, light it, and set the chimney in place. Clean the chimney and replace the oil as needed. Keep the lamp trimmed and burning and money will always be coming your way.

PROSPERI-TEA

This tea can be used as a drink, a floor wash, or a bath. (Of course, you should not drink it if you are allergic to any of the ingredients, so consult an herbalist or medical doctor if you are uncertain.) Blend 1 part Dandelion root, 1 part Burdock root, 1 part Yellow Dock root, 1 part Licorice root, 1/2 part Sarsaparilla, 1/2 part Cinnamon, and 1/2 part Ginger root. Using a teaspoon of herbs to a cup of water, brew it for fifteen minutes in boiling water as you recite your petition for financial success along with the 23rd Psalm. Make a cup at a time, or brew a pot full, strain it, sweeten it with honey, keep it in the refrigerator or freezer, and drink it cold or heated. Drink a cup every day for nine days, reciting your petition and the 23rd Psalm each day. Bathe with it and wash your entryway with it too, to draw in money.

MILK AND HONEY PROSPERITY BATH

The ancient luxury of a bath in milk and honey, made famous in tales of the Egyptian Queen Cleopatra, is a sensory delight and very soothing to the skin. "A land flowing with milk and honey" is a term used in the Bible more than 20 times to describe God's promise to free the Israelites from slavery in Egypt and deliver them to freedom in a place of verdant fertility, where they too could enjoy all that is nourishing and sweet in life.

Although the two main ingredients in the bath are milk and honey, it is customary when preparing it to add herbs and flowers for specific conditions — for instance, Rose petals and Juniper berries for a love bath or money herbs for bringing in prosperity. The choice of herbs is individual, based on preference and availability. You may consult the list of money herbs on page 15, use the Lucky Money Besamim herb mixture described below, or select Cinnamon for fast luck, whole Cloves and Calendula for gambling luck, Comfrey for money protection, Allspice berries for business income, or Five Finger Grass for the successful work of your hands.

Put six cups of milk in a saucepan with 2 cups of honey. Warm the milk slowly so you don't scald it. Add about a quarter-cup of the herbs, allow the herbs to steep in the milk and honey mixture for fifteen minutes, and strain them out. Draw a hot tub bath and pour this mixture into water. Take time in this bath, feel the luxury of it. Allow the milk and honey to absorb into your skin. When done in the bath let the water drain out and air dry, to allow all of the energies of your bath to further absorb into your skin.

LUCKY MONEY BESAMIM SPICES

In *"Hoodoo Bible Magic"* by Miss Michæle and Professor Porterfield we learn that "Besamim is a traditional spice mixture used every week by Jews at the Havdalah, a brief ceremony marking the formal conclusion to the Sabbath on Saturday nights. Specific ingredients and their number vary from maker to maker, but besamim is required to be fragrant, for its aroma is inhaled while praying thankfully to God for the creation of the 'varieties of spices.' In hoodoo, besamim has long been marketed as a Lucky Money Herb Mix and many people report that it is a powerful tool for drawing wealth. Mix together Cinnamon, Cloves, Myrtle, Hyssop, Rosemary, Anise, and Bay Leaf. You may inhale the scent, burn the mixture as incense, add it to a bath, dress money with it, or use it to roll candles in, while praying: *'Lord God who made the sweet perfumes, sweeten my money matters.'"*

AN ALL-PURPOSE MONEY ALTAR

From my book, *"Hoodoo Shrines and Altars"*:

"Build this altar during a waxing Moon or a full Moon, especially one that is associated with money, like the full Moon in Taurus. Dust the surface of your altar space with Money Drawing Sachet Powder. Over the top of the surface put a green altar cloth or an altar cloth that is covered with images of money. You may paper the altar with real dollar bills if you like.

"Get a small gold-coloured dish or tray and dress it with Money Stay With Me Oil, using a five-spot pattern. In the center, place a large lodestone. You can pile up a little 'nest' of coins around the lodestone. You will need to have magnetic sand as well, to feed your lodestone.

"Underneath the golden dish put a bill in the largest denomination that you can afford at that moment. Next, take a green pyramid candle and engrave your name on each of its four sides, also marking it with dollar signs above and below your name. Anoint two opposite sides of the pyramid with Money Drawing Oil and the other two sides with Money Stay With Me Oil.

"Each week burn some of the pyramid candle while you feed your lodestone with magnetic sand and place another bill beneath the golden dish. When the pyramid finishes burning, start another one. Keep this vigil going for as long as you want to keep the money coming in and staying in."

FIXING A SAND DOLLAR FOR THE MONEY ALTAR

The shell of a Sand Dollar is a natural curio often found at beaches, half buried in the sand. To replicate its power on your money altar, place a one dollar coin in a saucer, pour in a layer of magnetic sand, and wiggle the sand dollar into it, so that it looks as if you had just discovered it.

A ROSE OF JERICHO ON THE ALTAR

Place lucky fish-head rocks or other non-metallic wealth charms in a bowl of water with a dry Rose of Jericho. Water the plant, and as it comes back to life it will charge up the water and the items, bringing prosperity to your altar. Let the plant sit for no more than seven days, then allow it to dry out. Since the water it sat in is now charged with the magic of this plant, it can be used as a holy water, added to baths or floor washes. The curios can be added to mojo hands. Additionally, as the Rose of Jericho dries up again into a ball, you can slip a small money prayer, about the size of a Chinese fortune cookie paper, into its center, and it will hold onto it for you.

POT OF GOLD SPELL

Start with a beautiful bowl made from crystal or gold-tone metal. Pray over the bowl that it will hold the power of prosperity. Promise that you will take care of it, and you ask that in return, it will help with your financial needs. Put into it five dimes, a folded up two-dollar bill, and a small mirror.

Mix together a pinch of Nutmeg powder, a pinch of Cinnamon powder, a pinch of Five Finger Grass, and a pinch of pyrite grit. Sprinkle this over the items in the bowl, and on top of that, set a matched pair of "he" and "she" lodestones. Under the bowl place a petition paper with your wish written out. Feed the lodestones with magnetic sand and recite Psalms 23 on a daily basis. Every Tuesday offer your lodestones a little bit of whiskey and tell your money pot what money you will need for the coming week.

When the contents of the bowl loses scent, remove everything, set the solid objects back in place with fresh powders, and feed the lodestones. The old herb mix and magnetic sand can be scattered in your yard.

LODESTONE AND SILVER COINS WORN AT THE WAIST

Rev. Harry Hyatt learned this spell in 1939 from Informant #1116, a professional root doctor in Waycross, Georgia. She said, "Lodestone is a drawing power with your money. You place it with your money and you wear it around your waist with a dime or any silver piece of money. You put that lodestone around your waist and wear it, and it will bring you luck; you'll always have money."

THREE OF DIAMONDS: THREE COINS IN A FOUNTAIN

From Professor Charles Porterfield's book, *"A Deck of Spells"*:

"To gain wishes of happiness, money, or blessing, take the Three of Diamonds and write a wish for love, money, or blessing over each Diamond. Dress the card with 7-11 Holy Oil and Blessing Sachet Powder. Cut the card into three pieces so that each piece has a Diamond and a wish on it.

"Place the three card pieces into a plain envelope along with three silver dimes and three Mojo Beans. Pray the 33rd Psalm over the envelope each day for three days, and carry it in your pocket at all times. After the end of the three days go to a fountain, take one piece of the Three of Diamonds, one Mojo Bean, and one silver dime, and toss them over your left shoulder into the fountain while focusing on your wish. Repeat this for the next two days until all three wishes have gone into the fountain."

A LOADED GREEN PYRAMID CANDLE

Write your name nine times on square piece of paper, and around that, in a circle, write, *"Money, money come to me."* Put a pinch of Lucky Money Herbs Mix or your own favourite money herbs in the center of the paper. Fold or crumple the paper to make a small packet. Load a green pyramid candle by carving a hole in the bottom and setting aside the wax that you remove. Put your petition in the hole and melt the saved wax, then pour it into the hole to seal it. Dress the candle with Money Drawing Oil and dust it with Prosperity Sachet Powder. Set it on the center of a white plate or saucer. Surround it with Bayberry root chips, Sassafras chips, and pyrite grit. Recite the 23rd Psalm and light the candle to call in financial success and good luck.

HIDDEN MONEY TO SHARE THE BLESSINGS

I love this spell because it is all about paying it forward and sharing wealth. Dress nine one-dollar bills with Money Drawing Sachet Powder. Shake off the excess powder and snap each bill. Write a message such as *"Blessed with Prosperity"* on the bills with a green permanent marker. Once your bills are blessed, take them to town and strategically hide them where a stranger will find them and be blessed:
  • Tuck them in the pockets of clothes at a thrift or second-hand store.
  • Hide them between two cartons of milk at the grocery store.
  • Place them in the pages of books in a public library or a bookstore.

OLD-FASHIONED SYRUP RING SUCCESS CANDLE

Begin by acquiring an inexpensive white chinaware plate. It will be discarded at the close of the work, so shop for one at a thrift or second-hand store. Cleanse the plate with Hoyt's Cologne, and set it aside. Next, write out a money-drawing petition paper, and set it under the plate. Then, using a needle, inscribe your name and the success sigil ($$¢¢SS) into a 6-inch green candle, dress the candle with Money Drawing Oil, roll it in Cinnamon powder, and set it in the middle of plate. Encircle the candle with a ring of syrup. Sprinkle pyrite grit into the syrup while praying your money wishes out loud. Light the candle and allow it to burn down completely, but just before it goes out, pull out the petition paper and burn it to ash. When all is finished, carry the plate, with the spell remnants on it, to a crossroads and leave it there.

7 KNOB CANDLE FOR SEVEN-FOLD PROSPERITY

A green seven knob candle, burned one knob per day, will magnify your prosperity spell seven times. Start when the Moon is waxing and time the work so that the last knob burns on the night of the full Moon.

Inscribe "Prosperity" with dollar signs between each letter around each of the seven knobs of the candle, like this:

P $ R $ O $ S $ P $ E $ R $ I $ T $ Y $

On the back of a dollar bill or Chinese Hell Money, write a brief petition or scriptural prayer for prosperity. Dust the paper with Prosperity Sachet Powder, top it with a pile of Fenugreek seeds, and cover it with an overturned saucer. Dress the candle with Prosperity Oil and roll it in Alfalfa powder. Set the candle on the overturned saucer and circle it with seven coins. Light Prosperity Incense in a metal brazier, and after it is going well, light the candle and recite the 23rd Psalm. Let the candle burn one full knob, as you feel the prosperity coming to you. When it finishes, recite the 23rd Psalm again and snuff the candle out.

Each night, for the next six nights, light more incense and burn another candle knob. On the seventh night, when all is complete, gather up the leftover incense and incense ash, candle wax remains, remnant herbs, unused sachet, and your money petition. Wrap these into a packet and bury the packet under a plant or tree in your backyard or in the bottom of a potted plant that you keep towards the back of your house. As you do so, pray, *"As this plant grows, so will my money grow, seven-fold and more!"*

HIGH JOHN AND A SILVER DIME MOJO HAND

Dress a High John the Conqueror Root and a silver Mercury dime with Money Drawing Oil and fold a soft and worn two-dollar bill around them. Wind and tie this packet with green thread and sew it into a tight-fitting chamois cover. Feed it with Money Drawing Oil at least once a week.

HIGH JOHN AND DEVIL'S SHOE STRING MOJO HAND

In *"The Art of Making Mojos,"* Cat Yronwode describes a money hand made by wrapping a John the Conqueror Root, nine small Devil's Shoe Strings, and a silver Mercury dime from a leap year date in a two-dollar bill. The packet goes in a green bag dressed with Van Van Oil. This mojo draws money, boosts personal power, and enhances charisma. Carry it when gambling or keep it by the front door of your business to call in customers.

SPELLS TO KEEP YOUR MONEY

Getting the money you need is only half the challenge. Once you've got it, you have to hold onto it. Many people think of keeping money in terms of physical protection, such as hiding your cash from thieves, but for those who look at the full picture, there is an interesting added dimension to money-keeping magic. This consists of simply not having things go wrong. If your roof does not leak, your shoulder does not need surgery, your car does not break down, and your phone is not lost, you won't have to spend money, and you will have, in effect, saved money.

MONEY STAY: THE MAGIC OF DELAY

In *"The Spirit of Black Hawk"* by Jason Berry, a clear description is given of what Rev. Harry M. Hyatt called "the magic of delay":

"And we know from Black Hawk that we have to be careful about our money," continued the celebrant. *"We have to use our money carefully. Can't waste money. And you —" His voice was gentle now, as he faced a little lady in the front pew— "I know you been worried about money."*

She nodded.

"And you need money."

"Yes, Lawd," she said softly.

"All right now, The money is coming. But you have to wait. But the money is coming. Now, when the money comes, it will be a check in the mail. And you leave that check up on yo' bureau. When it comes, no matter how much you need that money, you leave it on the bureau, and wait five days before you spend it."

The above speech came out of the Spiritual Church Movement in New Orleans, but, from Mister Felix in Columbus, Georgia, to Miss Cat in Forestville, California, you will find root doctors and spiritual ministers advising clients and congregants to pause before spending their income.

"Something happens when you hold back from spending, even for a few days or a week," says Miss Cat. "You create a sort of spiritual dam, and the money piles up behind that dam, and it accumulates. When you finally release the funds, they come out with greater force and go farther. So many people have told me this, that i have come to believe that it is a true spiritual principle. I teach it, and i use it myself."

COOKING WITH THYME FOR MONEY PROTECTION

To continually work money protection, all it takes is the addition of a pinch of Thyme into your food with the recitation of Psalms 150 three times. This trick is better when your meal is savoury, but a little pinch of Thyme can work in sweet foods too. If you have a green thumb, grow a Thyme plant by your kitchen door and watch your money grow.

COMFREY IN YOUR WALLET OR SAVINGS PASSBOOK

Comfrey herb works to help you hold on to your money, while also keeping it safe and protected. Place a Comfrey leaf that has been dressed with Money Stay With Me Oil in your wallet to help your money stay with you. This is especially helpful when you are trying to not spend money or use your credit cards. The Comfrey will also protect your wallet from being stolen. If you grow Comfrey, use a fresh leaf to begin and watch as the leaf dries out. When the leaf becomes so brittle that it starts to crumble and fall apart, replace it with a new one.

Another way to use a Comfrey leaf to save money is to open a savings account, no matter how small, and have the bank give you an old fashioned passbook. Place a Comfrey leaf in the passbook as a book mark.

FINANCIAL PROTECTION MOJO FROM LOU FLOREZ

"Start by creating an anointing oil. Mix three pinches of salt with a dram of Olive Oil and let this sit for nine days. During these nine days, pray over the oil at sunrise with the intention of reversing misfortune and protecting your finances and money-luck.

"After the nine days make your mojo. You will need a red flannel bag, a petition paper, nine Grains of Paradise seeds, Lamb's Ear herb, a blue anil ball, and a Mercury dime. Start with the petition paper and anoint the four corners and middle of the paper with the prayed-over Olive Oil. Speak your petition aloud and spit into the middle of the paper. Fold that paper three times away from yourself and place it in the red flannel bag. Next you will work with each of the ingredients individually. Take each item and pray over it as you did with the Olive Oil, anoint it with the blessed oil, and spit on it before placing it in the red flannel bag. Finally, tie the mojo, bring it to life by following the prayer-anoint-spit formula that you used for each of the ingredients, and then keep it with you to protect your finances."

MONEY STAY WITH ME SPELL FROM CAT YRONWODE

"If you have money coming in, but find it hard to build up savings or meet your monthly bills, you may need a Money Stay With Me Spell to slow down your spending and allow cash reserves to accumulate. Remember: 'It's not how much you get, it's how much you can hold on to!'

"You will need a green seven knob candle, a large lodestone, magnetic sand, Money Stay With Me Incense Powder, Money Stay With Me Sachet Powder, Money Stay With Me Oil, four silver dimes, your name on paper, and a personal concern, such as your trimmed fingernails. This spell takes seven days, but once you start, you can continue as long as you like. Set everything up on top of a bureau and store the tray, candle, and dimes in a drawer during the daytime, to keep the money out of sight.

"Lay your name paper and your concerns on the tray, with the lodestone on top. Inscribe each knob of the candle, *'Money Stay With Me.'* Dress the candle with oil. Place the dimes around the foot of the candle in the form of a cross. Light some incense, then the candle. Now be honest with yourself. It's not how much you get, it's how much you can hold on to. Dig into your pockets or purse and pull out all your cash. Yes, even the cash hidden in your sock drawer. Put the change and any bill under $20.00 denomination back. Write your name on each bill worth $20.00 or more. Dress the four corners of each bill with oil and dust it with sachet powder. Place the bills under the lodestone, neatly stacked, facing East to West on top of your name paper. Say aloud, *'Money Stay With Me,'* and feed the lodestone a pinch of magnetic sand. Let the candle burn one knob, and put it out.

"The next night do everything as before, but stack the money criss-cross, with the new bills facing North to South. Do this every night for seven nights, criss-crossing the bills. Any night when you don't have bills worth $20.00 or more, use the bills you have of highest denomination. On the seventh night, the bills at the bottom of the stack are yours to spend.

"Tie the dimes, remnant wax, and incense ashes in red cloth, and bury them near your front door. The lodestone is now trained to keep your money. Put it in the drawer on its tray. Every night sign and dress all your bills worth $20.00 or more and criss-cross them under the lodestone, then take old bills from the bottom of the stack. Spend the trained money and replace it with new bills daily so the lodestone is always keeping more money for you. As time goes by, you will find more and more $20.00 bills on the tray. If the stack gets too high, start in again with $100.00 dollar bills."

ALKANET TO PROTECT YOUR MONEY

Alkanet is said to keep money safe from theft. Make Alkanet Oil by letting the bark flakes sit a week in a small bottle of Olive Oil. Dress coins with the oil and bury them face-up at the outside corners of your house.

LOCKING UP YOUR CASH TO KEEP IT WITH YOU

Cat Yronwode shares her savings secret: "Purchase a simple dial-face combination padlock, a length of matching lightweight steel chain, and a wooden box large enough to hold unfolded currency. The lock will come with a multi-digit numerical code to open it. Memorize the combination and NEVER use those numbers to bet the lottery, ever, ever, ever.

"Oil the box, inside and out, with Money Stay With Me Oil and Magnet Oil. On a piece of U.S. currency or Chinese Spirit Money, write the total amount of money you intend to accumulate and your purpose for saving it, such as for a new car or computer, a vacation, or the down payment on a house. Place the petition in the box and pray that all the money added to this box will be only used for the purpose you have declared. Place a dollar in seed money in the box, wrap the chain around it and padlock it.

"Every night, as you empty your pockets, pull out a bill of any denomination, unlock the padlock, undo the chain, and add the bill. Once a week, dress the outside of the box with the two oils and take a moment to change out any five ones in the box for a five, any two fives for a ten, any two tens for a twenty, and any five twenties for a hundred. You can go to the bank to get the hundreds if they do not come to you — and you will need to, because soon enough, the box will be full, and all you will have room for is hundreds. When the box can hold no more hundreds, put it away in a safe place and start another box.

"And always remember, 'You can make it if you try!'"

TWO-DOLLAR BILL MONEY PROTECTION SPELL

Dust a new and crisp two-dollar bill with Money Stay With Me Sachet Powder and Money Drawing Sachet Powder. Snap it between your fingers to remove any excess powder, then anoint it in a five-spot pattern with Protection Oil, placing a dot of oil on each corner and at the center. Place this bill in your money clip or wallet. It will work to keep the rest of your money safe, keep you from over-spending, and bring more cash into your pocket. Reapply the powders and oil at every full Moon.

Spells to Get Out of Debt

Sometimes, for reasons we were not able to control at the time, we find ourselves having to deal with debts from the past. Whether it's an old student loan, the fallout from a bad divorce, a misguided business venture, an unexpected medical expense, or a thoughtless bout of credit card spending, getting out of debt may require more than mundane methods.

REDUCING DEBT AS THE MOON WANES

Start by making a list of all of the debts that you have and to whom they are owed. This may take you some time. Look up all the account numbers and write down the monetary totals. Include everything: mortgages, back rent, credit cards, bank fees, medical bills, personal loans, tax bills, car loans, alimony, child support payments, bills in arrears, and overdue monthly charges for utilities and insurance payments. When you have all your debts listed you may start to feel the weight of your debts as a heavy load upon you, but don't let that stop you. You are starting now to make changes to reduce your debts.

Set up an altar by dusting the surface of a small table with Wealthy Way Sachet Powder. Lay a green altar cloth down over this, and place your list of debts right in the center of the space. Create a crossroads of magnetic sand on top of your paper. Along the North-South axis of the four roads, place two green glass-encased candles, and along the East-West axis, place two yellow-gold glass-encased candles. Dress and bless all four with Wealthy Way Oil, plus crumbled Comfrey leaf and Alfalfa.

Begin at the full Moon and keep the candles lit every day until the New Moon. Burn them continuously, praying that as the Moon wanes and vanishes, so too will your debts be reduced. As each candle is consumed, start a new one in its place. On the night of the new Moon, blow out any candles still burning, burn the list of debts, mix the burnt paper ashes with the magnetic sand from the crossroads you created and take down your altar. Dispose of the remains at a crossroads.

Then, as the Moon waxes, follow up on this working with real world action. Cut up your credit cards, make payment plans, talk to a debt consolidation service, and carry out all the necessary mundane activities that will support the rootwork that you've done.

PROSPER BY PAYING YOUR BILLS WITH GRATITUDE

Always be grateful that you have the money to pay your bills, knowing that as you make that payment the money is coming back to you.

If you write checks to pay your bills, dust the checks with Prosperity Sachet Powder. In the memo line of each check write *"Thank you"* or *"Grateful."* This sets up a reciprocal energy between your payment and the Divine, and will affect those who touch or handle the checks.

If you pay your bills online, anoint your fingers with Prosperity Oil before logging in to your accounts. In the memo line of the payment you make online, type out *"Thank you"* or *"Grateful,"* if possible.

If your bills are paid by automatic withdrawal, make a note of the day the funds will be withdrawn, anoint your fingers with Prosperity Oil and pray Psalms 23 with gratitude.

PSALMS 37 TO GET AN EXTENSION ON OVERDUE RENT

Mix four parts Tobacco snuff with one part each of Chia Seeds and red brick dust. Put this in a narrow-necked bottle, and pray sincerely over it Psalms 37:3 *("Trust in the Lord, and do good; so shalt thou dwell in the land, and verily thou shalt be fed")*. Walk around your home praying this verse repeatedly, and when you return to your front door, pour the mix out in a line across the threshold. Having done this, apply for a job, approach your boss for extra hours, or find a second job to bring in more income.

PUT YOUR CREDIT CARDS ON ICE

Take out all of your credit cards and lay them on your kitchen table. Cut a credit-card-sized paper for each of the cards, named and numbered as the cards are, and on each paper write the balance due on that card. Stack up the papers, light some Crucible of Courage Incense, and burn the papers one by one in the incense. Mix the ashes from the papers with Money Stay With Me Sachet Powder. Anoint a 4-inch green candle with Money Stay With Me Oil and roll it in the mixed sachet powder and ashes. Write a petition paper with the words *"I will pay off my credit card bills,"* signed with your name, and lay it under the candle. Recite Psalms 61 *("Hear my cry, O God; attend unto my prayer")* while you light the candle. As it burns, pick up all of your credit cards, put them into a coffee cup, and half fill the cup with water. Place the cup in your freezer, repeat Psalms 61, and leave it there. Forever. When your credit cards are paid off, switch to using debit cards only.

KEEP YOUR PENNIES SEPARATE FROM YOUR SILVER

It is a widespread folk belief that if you want to prosper, you should keep your copper pennies separate from your silver money. Some people take this advice a step farther and add that you should not bother to count your pennies, for to do so is small-minded and petty.

In October 1939, Harry Hyatt was in Memphis, Tennessee, interviewing Black root doctors in the private home of Mrs. Jones, when a worker who was noted as Informant #1524 explained it this way: "If I got silver money, I counts my silver, but I hardly ever counts my pennies. I keeps my silver money specially separate from my pennies. Well, now, I go to trade my pennies for silver, if I got pennies. Why, I'll take my pennies and use them all as far as they go, but I never mix my pennies with my silver money."

The following spell is founded on the same old-school prosperity belief:

Start on your pay day. You will need two large glass jars with lids and two pieces of petition paper. The first petition is a wish, such as *"May I save [dollar amount] by [date]."* Write your savings account number along the four edges of this paper. The second petition is the text of Deuteronomy 15:7: *"If there be among you a poor man of one of thy brethren within any of thy gates in thy land which the Lord thy God giveth thee, thou shalt not harden thine heart, nor shut thine hand from thy poor brother."*

Create two small mojos in matching squares of green fabric. Each will contain a small lodestone, three Juniper berries, three Cloves, Peppermint, Alfalfa, and Cinnamon chips. Put your wish-petition and a silver coin in one mojo and the scriptural passage and a penny in the other. Tie the mojo hands and put one into each jar. Go through your home and gather up all of the loose change that you can find. Sort the coins, placing all the pennies in the penny-mojo jar and all the silver coins in the wish-mojo jar.

On your next pay day again gather up all your change and sort the coins into the two jars. Feed your jars with a small pinch of magnetic sand and recite Psalms 150. It is important that you do not spend any change on your pay day before sorting your coins; break dollar bills instead.

When the jar of silver coins is full, take it to the bank and deposit it, even if it's only a few dollars. That trained money will help your savings account to grow. When the jar of pennies is full, give them away as an offering to the world, so that all may share in your abundance. One way that my friend Nagasiva Yronwode does this is by throwing pennies over his left shoulder in grocery store parking lots, for strangers to find as lucky coins.

BLESS YOURSELF TO GET OUT OF DEBT

On a Saturday as the Moon is waning, light a 9-inch white jumbo candle dressed with Blessing Oil. Total up your debts, write the total on a small paper, put Hyssop and salt on the the paper for forgiveness, crumple it into a ball, wrap it in Knot Weed to tie it down, and put it under an overturned plate. Dress a 4-inch black candle with Van Van Oil to turn bad to good, light it, and set it atop the plate. Sit with the black candle as it burns. Snuff out the blessing candle and set it aside. Bury the paper-ball at a crossroads.

At the full Moon re-light the jumbo blessing candle. On a paper, write the total needed to pay off your debts. Put a pinch each of Five Finger Grass, Fenugreek seeds, and lodestone grit on it to draw help. Fold it toward yourself and put it under an overturned plate. Dress a 4-inch green candle with Money Drawing Oil, light it, and set it atop the plate. Recite the 23rd Psalm and sit with the green candle as it burns. When it is finished, snuff out the Blessing candle. Take this paper to running water and throw it in.

IF IN ARREARS, PREVENT FORECLOSURE OR EVICTION

To buy time while you refinance a mortgage or make a payment plan for overdue rent, get a railroad spike for every corner of your property. Dress them with Protection and House Blessing Oils. Pray over them with Psalms 15 (*"Lord, who shall abide in thy tabernacle?"*). Hammer a spike into every corner of your land. Cover the head of each spike with graveyard dirt, ideally from one of your ancestors. If that isn't possible, get dirt from a grave with your birth surname. If that isn't possible, chose a grave that calls to you.

Urinate along the property line to mark your territory. You can do this right on the ground or collect your urine and sprinkle it as you walk the line.

SAINT ANTHONY HELPS THE POOR

In 1940 in Algiers, Louisiana, Rev. Hyatt talked with Informant #1577, a Catholic worker who shared a blessing for those in poverty. She told him, "Saint Anthony is for children and for the poor. You pray to St. Anthony for work or for bread. Use brown candles, on Tuesdays and Thursdays. If you're out of a job, you pray to him to help you to get a job. If you have children and you want bread in your home, you pray to him for that bread. You make him a promise, that when you get what you asked for, you'll go to a Catholic church where they have a St. Anthony's box and put money in his box for the poor. But you mustn't promise him that and not give it to him."

SPELLS FOR REAL ESTATE AND TENANCY

Shelter is among our most basic needs, and whether we are renting, buying, or selling, it is almost a certainty that money will be involved.

A MAP FOR FINDING, RENTING, OR BUYING A HOME
This is a traditional spell with a modern technological twist. In times past, we used paper street maps and photos; these days, everything is online.

Print a map of the area to which you are trying to relocate. You may start with a state, county, city, or neighbourhood. Write a petition on the map, such as, *"May I move to Maryland and be content," "I shall find and purchase an 80 acre farm in Oregon County, Missouri,"* or *"Dear Lord, help me buy a home within a ten-minute walk of my shop."* Collect some dirt from the state, county, city, or neighbourhood. If you can get it from the four corners of the map area, so much the better, but any dirt will do. Lay a silver coin on each corner of the map. Dress a yellow candle with House Blessing Oil, Van Van Oil, and Crown of Success Oil. Sprinkle both the candle and the map with the dirt you collected. Pray for your desire and light the candle.

As you close in on a specific place, add a new map, dirt, and coins atop the previous one. When you have one home in mind, print a street-view photo of the building and collect dirt from the yard. Write your petition on the photo, including the address, how much you want to pay, and any special terms you need out of the deal. At each corner of the photo place a silver coin and a railroad spike. Dress, sprinkle, pray over, and light the candle as before. When it finishes, go to the place and nail the spikes in the dirt at each corner of the house, to nail down the property for yourself. This will have to be done covertly.

Make a folded packet out of each map and the photo. Into each packet put that paper's four coins and dirt, plus powdered Cloves, Comfrey, and Five Finger Grass. In the packet made from the photo of the home, also add the names or business cards of any people involved with the transaction, such as a real estate agent, seller of the house, loan officer, or housing agency. Put these in a jar of honey and burn yellow candles dressed with House Blessing Oil and Crown of Success Oil on the jar. Light one candle daily on the jar until the purchase or rental is complete and you have the keys to your new home. Bury the jar in the backyard or in a potted plant.

HOUSE-GETTING PRAYER TO OUR LADY OF LORETO

This Catholic prayer to rent or buy housing comes from Aura Laforest:
"Our Lady of Loreto, I implore your Holy Name. Help me find a home with the aid of your Holy Son our Lord Jesus Christ and your Holy Husband Saint Joseph. For the sake of the peace and joy in your Holy House of Loreto, where you lived happily by the grace and blessing that the Holy Father granted you, I implore you spiritually to help me as I concentrate on my future home. Holy Mother of Loreto, grant us health, peace, and happiness, and help us in our lives. Just as your house was holy and blessed by God, I ask that my future home be blessed and protected by you and by God. If you help me, Holy Virgin, and grant my request [state your request here], I will magnify your name, and my friends will also bless you."

SPELL TO HAVE YOUR HOUSE BID WIN OVER OTHERS

For this working you will need a 9-inch purple jumbo candle. Carve the address of the house and your name into the wax. Dress the candle with I Can You Can't Oil. Make a petition paper with the address written nine times and your named crossed over it nine times. Around the criss-cross block of names, write in a circle *"This is my house"* repeatedly, without taking your pen off of the paper. Set this under the candle and light it.

While the candle burns, put together a sugar or honey jar with the names of the sellers inside, so they will favour you above all others. Add a little Deer's Tongue herb to this, so they will pay attention to your offer.

Finally, get some dirt from the house and mix it with I Can, You Can't Sachet Power. As you mix it, voice your desire, something like this: *"All others are unable to make an offer on this house, all other offers fall through, no one can compete with me. I can do what others can't."* Take the dirt back to the house and sprinkle it in the front yard or along the path leading up to the front door, repeating your prayer as you go.

MONEY LUCK AND PROTECTION FOR THE HOME

In her book *"Women's Work,"* Aura Laforest shares a simple money house blessing: "Put a piece of Black Snake Root and a piece of lodestone grit in a small bottle of Hoyt's Cologne, carry it on your person for three days so that it picks up your essence, and then bury the bottle upright in the ground near your doorstep with a coin placed face-up on top of the cap. You can lightly cover the coin with a leaf, so it will not be seen."

SUGAR BOX FOR SECTION 8 APPROVAL

This spell was written by Miss Cat for her clients:

"Some modern workers advise clients to treat subsidised housing cases as if folks wanted to move into a new apartment or house. However, there is an additional issue with such cases, namely the bureaucracy and red tape associated with governmental assistance — and we do have a hoodoo heritage of spells for breaking through governmental and bureaucratic logjams, so let us put the two ways of working together and come up with a spell for unlocking your Section 8 Housing. In doing this work, you will call upon God's help and ask for compassion from specific people, in an attempt to get someone at the housing agency to act on your behalf.

"Write your caseworker's name on an image of the agency's logo or, better yet, on the caseworker's business card, and place it in the bottom of a sugar bowl, a one-pint Mason jar, or a one-pound sugar box. Into your sugar, mix a pinch each of Cinnamon powder (for money and for 'heat' on the agency), Allspice powder (for money), Clove powder (for friendship and for money), and powdered Five Finger Grass (for the granting of favours). Use only enough spice and herb powder in the sugar to speckle it, not to discolour it, because you will be cooking with it and eating it.

"Get a house key. I prefer the old-fashioned skeleton key type, but any key will do. Pour the doctored sugar into the jar or box, on top of the caseworker's name. Insert the key into the sugar, as you would stick a key into a lock in a door. Turn the key, as if you were opening the locked door, while saying Psalms 23 (*'The Lord is my shepherd ...'*). Do this three times a day, all at once or at intervals, such as 6:00 AM, Noon, and 6:00 PM.

"Every day, at least once, taste some of the sugar, flavour your coffee or tea with it, or cook with it, saying, *'As this sugar is sweet to me, so will [Name] (or [the agency]) be sweet to me and favour my case above all others, coming to my assistance with care, concern, and alacrity.'* Call aloud the caseworker's name and the Golden Rule from Luke 6:31 (*'And as ye would that men should do to you, do ye also to them likewise. Amen.'*)

As the sugar is taken out, replace it occasionally with new doctored sugar. Keep this going until you are approved for housing. When you are approved, use all the sugar to bake a cake or a batch of cookies and distribute the sweet treats to anyone who also needs financial assistance of some kind. Dispose of the petition paper by carrying it to your new home and burying it in the ground or in a potted plant there, with thanks."

HOW TO EXCHANGE BAD TENANTS FOR GOOD

In March 1938, Rev. Hyatt met a man he called "The Diviner of Candles" in New Orleans. The Diviner told how to drive off bad tenants and bring in good ones: "Well, you could get you some new wine and get you some· Mustard seed, and go to a graveyard and get you some dirt off a grave; and mix that up together and carry it and sprinkle it right down before the door there, and it won't be but a short while before they'll be moved. [Then] you could take you some Frankincense and some brown sugar, and mix that up together in a bottle of ammonia and scrub your house out with it early in the morning, just about sunrise. And take some of that Frankincense and burn it in there. That's for drawing power. You'll soon have your house rented."

MEMPHIS BOARDING HOUSE FLOOR WASH

In 1938, in Memphis, Tennessee, Harry Hyatt collected quite a number of recipes for spiritual supply formulas. This floor wash to bring in tenants was shared with him by Informant #928, a hoodoo lady who also ran a boarding house. Hyatt's questions to her are in parentheses:

"I run a boarding house. I got Oil of Bergamine [Bergamot], Oil of Cinnamon, Oil of Rose, and Oil of Wintergreen. I pour it in a ten-cent bottle [a small perfume bottle, used as a measure of the combined oils], and I would put it into as much water as the size of bucket that I was going to use to mop my house, and then add Ivory Soap chips or either a brand-new bar of Ivory Soap that haven't been used anywheres. I'd start from my front steps and mop straight back, and mop inward all over my house back to the back step, to the very bottom step. And it would bring a crowd and bring just whatever you would want for the purpose. And I'd do that on Mondays and Fridays early in the morning.

"When I wanted men transient trade, I would let a man urinate in my scrub water. Get enough of it to mop my house through with that other, you see — Oil of Cinnamon and Oil of Rose, Oil of Bergamine and Oil of Wintergreen, and Ivory Soap — and I usually wanted male trade more than I did the female, so I just, I might get a young half-grown boy or something, and just let him, when I fix my water bucket, he use it."

(Get any male water?)

"That's it."

(Well, what about women? What do you bring them in with?)

"If you want female roomers, you'd get a woman to urinate in the water."

TWO GREEN CANDLES TO ATTRACT GOOD TENANTS

When your old tenants leave, wash the front sidewalk, path, hall, or doorway with nine successive buckets of water, to each of which you have added a dash of ammonia. Mop or sweep inward, toward the front door, the whole time. When you are finished, sprinkle the area closest to the door with powdered Cinnamon and sugar, to draw sweet renters with money to spend.

Fix a green candle for your property inscribed with the address and the word *"Welcome!"* Dress it with Attraction Oil. Print out a photo of the place and set it under the candle. Next, fix a green candle for the new tenants inscribed with a phrase like *"Ideal tenant."* Dress it with Cedar Wood Oil. Write out the characteristics of your perfect tenant — do they have children or pets, how much money do they make, are they mature, how long do you want them to stay? Place this paper under the tenants' candle.

For seven days burn the candles in sections, moving the tenants' candle closer to the property candle each time. On the last day bring the candles together, so they are touching, and let them burn out. Bury any remains in the front yard; if there isn't a yard, use a potted plant near the front door.

CEDAR WOOD TO RENT OUT ROOMS

Over at the Lucky Mojo Forum, Miss Cat shared this information:

"Herbs for property rental include Cedar Wood (housing), Cinnamon (money), Cloves (friendly people, money), sugar (nice and sweet people), and magnetic sand (to attract and draw what you want). Essential oils include those from all of the herbs named, plus Bergamot (to influence others). These can be blended into spiritual supplies of various kinds — but if you only have one thing, then the most traditional of all the herbs employed for property rental is Cedar Wood.

"Depending on the type of property and its situation, the Cedar Wood may be in the form of chips, oil, sachet powders, incense, and so forth. To rent out a room in a boarding house, you may anoint the door knobs of the room with Cedar Wood Oil while speaking your prayer. Prospective tenants will touch the door knobs and pick up the power that you and the Cedar Wood have conveyed thereby. To rent a detached home on a lot, you might wish to line the path with Cedar Wood chips or Cedar Wood Incense Powder mixed into the dirt, but still put the Cedar Wood Oil on every doorknob and pray over each doorknob that the place be rented — and be sure to state what kind of a renter you want."

SAINT JOSEPH TO SELL A HOUSE

This spell was written by Cat Yronwode, based on traditional sources:

"When selling a house, it is up to you to see that the premises are clean and that the asking price is within market value. You will need a Saint Joseph Vigil Candle, a statuette of Saint Joseph, a bottle of Saint Joseph Oil, a Saint Joseph chromo print, and a Saint Joseph holy card.

"Dress the candle with Saint Joseph Oil, Cedar, Cinnamon, and Cloves. As it burns, hang the print of Saint Joseph where it will be seen by those who are viewing the house. Hide the holy card of Saint Joseph among your real estate papers (deed, termite inspection notice, mortgage, etc.). Spray or dab Saint Joseph Oil in the four corners of each room, each window frame, each door jamb, and the framed print. When you are done with this, hold the statue of Saint Joseph in the your hand as you recite the following:

"O, Saint Joseph, you who taught our Lord the carpenter's trade, and saw to it that he was always properly housed, hear my earnest plea. I want you to help me now as you helped your foster-child Jesus, and as you have helped many others in the matter of housing. I wish to sell this house quickly, easily, and profitably and I implore you to grant my wish by bringing me a good buyer, one who is eager, compliant, and honest, and by letting nothing impede the rapid conclusion of the sale.

"Dear Saint Joseph, I know you would do this for me out of the goodness of your heart and in your own good time, but my need is very great now and so I must make you hurry on my behalf.

"Saint Joseph, I am going to place you in a difficult position with your head in darkness and you will suffer as our Lord suffered, until this house is sold. Then, Saint Joseph, I swear before the cross and God Almighty, that I will redeem you and you will receive my gratitude and a place of honour in my home. Amen.

"Take up the statue of Saint Joseph and dig a hole in your back yard. If there is no back yard, use the front yard. If there is no yard at all, dig a hole in a large potted plant. Bury the statue upside down, head downward, facing east, in the hole and cover it over. Let the candle burn continually inside until it goes out.

"When the property sells, you must dig up the statue, clean it, and carry it with you to your new home, where it should be kept in a place of honour. Failure to do this will lead to trouble with the sale or trouble with the new home or property."

Spells for Getting a Job

Having gainful employment is one of the most obvious ways to make money. However, having the right job, the best job, the job that makes you the happiest — a good job that you like — can make for a really great life.

HIRE ME CANDLE SPELL

Print out the job you desire on a piece of paper before you submit an application or resume. Write your name nine times on the paper and place it under a glass-encased yellow candle dressed with Steady Work Oil. Keep the light burning until you receive your job offer. Anoint your fingers with Steady Work Oil and submit your resume. As you hit the "send" button, recite Psalms 23. When you go to the interview, anoint yourself with Steady Work Oil before leaving the house, and keep your candle burning at home.

SALT AND GRAVEL ROOT FOR LANDING A JOB

Salt will help you get a job, if you are stealthy. Before going for an interview put a handful of salt in your pocket. While there, try to get some of the salt on your potential boss's clothing without being seen. If you are able to achieve this you will get the job and always be treated well by your employer. If you are caught, all bets are off. Similarly, you can mix ground-up Gravel Root with salt and sprinkle it where the boss will step.

FROM A DIME TO A DOLLAR TO GET HIRED

In 1939 in Savannah, Georgia, a worker known as Informant #1276 told Rev. Hyatt the job-getting spell she taught to her own clients: "Start this right with a dime. You can do this with any coin from a dime to a dollar. To do the work, you get a half pint of the very best gin liquor that you can buy. Take a sewing thimble and you pour a sewing thimble full of Hoyt's Cologne into that half pint of gin liquor, and that amount of money, from a dime on up to a dollar, you let it soak there overnight in that half pint of gin liquor. And you put that coin into your right pocket and you go before the boss the next morning. The real fact about it, sir, you may have to make three trips. You may make three trips before he makes any oath [or promise], before he gives you the job." If the first interview goes well, increase the denomination of the coin for each successive interview until you are hired.

PUT THE INTERVIEWER IN YOUR SHOE

Write the name of the person who will be interviewing you nine times. Write your name across theirs nine times in a criss-cross pattern. Encircle the name-block with your desire written over and over, like, *"hire me hire me hire me."* Put a five-spot of Crown of Success Oil on the petition paper. Add a pinch each of sugar, salt, and Gravel Root in the middle. Fold the paper into a packet and tuck it into your left shoe. Dust the bottoms of your shoes with Steady Work Sachet Powder before leaving home.

HAND POWDER FOR A SUCCESSFUL INTERVIEW

Before your meeting, sprinkle Attraction Sachet Powder and Steady Work Sachet Powder into your hand. State your wish out loud: *"[Name], you will hire me and offer me the salary I want."* Clap your hands three times to get off the powder. Go in and shake hands! This spell works in any situation where you want to make a good impression — just switch out the Steady Work Powder for any other condition powder, as desired.

ACE OF CLUBS: TO HELP GET STEADY WORK

This comes to us from Professor Porterfield's *"A Deck of Spells"*:

"If you need steady work, get a white crucifix candle, two blue offertory candles, and the Ace of Clubs. Draw a dollar sign ($) in the two blank corners of the card, sign your name at its top, and write the words *"Steady Work"* over and over across the card until it is filled. Dress the candles and card with Steady Work Oil. Place a pinch of Gravel Root or Steady Work Sachet Powder on top of the Ace of Clubs, place an overturned white saucer over it, and set the crucifix candle on top of the saucer. Place the three candles in a row, with the blue ones to either side of the crucifix candle. Light all three candles, pick up the blue offertory candles in your hands, pray the 23rd Psalm aloud, and ask for a job. Replace the blue candles to their previous places and let all the candles burn until they go out.

"When you leave for a job interview, take the Ace of Clubs from beneath the saucer and place it inside your right shoe along with the name of the company or the business card of your interviewer, so that you will "walk on them" during the interview. Keep a Steady Work vigil light candle dressed with Gravel Root and Steady Work Oil burning at home in a safe place while you are at the interview. Carry some Gravel Root and a pinch of salt in your pocket, and look the interviewer in the eye as you speak."

CAT'S "PAPER IN YOUR SHOE FOR A JOB INTERVIEW"

"This job is done for a client by a root doctor, and it was shown to me by a worker who knew her business, but i have taught others to do it for themselves. I will describe it as if you were helping a client and i trust you to make the necessary changes if you are doing the work for yourself.

"Stand the client barefoot with her right foot upon a piece of paper if she is right-handed. If she is left-handed, stand her with her left foot on the paper. The best paper is tough, unprinted grocery sack paper, unless — and this is important — the job she wants is with a retail store that packages customers' goods in its own imprinted bags. As i was told, 'If you want a job as a cashier at the Piggly Wiggly, get a paper bag from the Piggly Wiggly and stand right on their name, but if you want a job from the hardware store, go in and buy something and get one of their paper bags and stand right on that. Even if they use plain paper bags, stand on a bag that came from that store, if you want a position in that store.'

"Those instructions date from the 1970s, and since then i have added to this old method the idea that if the company is not a retail outlet, but does have an internet presence, you should print out a corporate web page with the company logo on it, especially a page that relates to the job you want.

"Kneel down and trace around the client's foot with a pencil. Pray for the client as you do this. Cut out the shape of her foot, inside the line so that the paper is smaller than her actual foot and will fit in her shoe. On the paper, write out Luke 11:9, but insert the client's name and the name of the company in the scripture, so it looks like this:

And I say unto you,
Betty Ann Ransome Lewis,
Ask, and it shall be given you,
By the Piggly Wiggly in Jackson, Mississippi;
Seek, and ye shall find,
A job as a cashier or in the warehouse, either one;
Knock, and it shall be opened unto you,
In Jesus' name, Amen.

"Draw dollar signs all around this prayerful petition and dress the paper with Steady Work Oil in the form of a cross. Tell the client to wear the paper in her shoe as she goes to the interview. Have her call you when the interview is scheduled so that you can keep a yellow light dressed with Steady Work Oil going for the date and time of the interview."

CAT'S "PAPER UNDER A CANDLE FOR A JOB INTERVIEW"

"The same woman who showed me the previous spell gave the advice that the client was to be given a bottle of Steady Work Oil to bathe with and to rub the oil on her hands before meeting the interviewer at the job site. I followed her lead and told it this way for years. This was not a spell involving the use of papers, so i would not have included it here except as a footnote to the previous page, a mere add-on to the footprint spell.

"However, when the book *'Hoodoo Bible Magic'* by Miss Michæle and Professor Charles Porterfield came out in 2014, i saw that they had coupled the same scripture i used (Luke 11:9) to another verse (Psalms 90:17), and this gave me the idea to couple their second verse to the second portion of the footprint spell, which involved the hand-treatment. So this is an example of how rootworkers influence one another over the years.

"Miss Michæle and Professor Porterfield recommended Psalms 90:17 as a paper for the shoe, but the verse does not mention feet; rather it specifies the hands. The woman from Jackson, Mississippi, had taught me a hand-treatment, but she had given me no scripture for that portion of her work. Putting two and two together, i devised the following:

"Trace the client's right hand if right-handed or left hand if left-handed onto a piece of paper. See the previous spell for how this should be done. Cut out the handprint and on it write Psalms 90:17: *'And let the beauty of the Lord our God be upon us: and establish thou the work of our hands upon us; yea, the work of our hands establish thou it.'*

"Have the client sign the scriptural passage with her full name.

"Open a small bottle of Steady Work Oil for her and pray this scripture over her hand as you dress the palm of her hand liberally with the oil, then place her hand down into her handprint to mark the hand outline as hers. Place the handprint paper face-up under a candle stand. Inscribe her name into the yellow candle (mentioned in the previous spell) which you will set as her job interview candle on the day and at the time she tells you to set it. Dress the candle with Steady Work Oil and give her the remainder of the bottle, with instructions to add a few drops to her bath and to anoint her hands with the oil as she says the portion of scripture every day up to and including the day of the interview.

"I hope that you have enjoyed this glimpse into how an old, experienced worker such as myself creatively crafts spiritual patchwork from donated scraps. This one is a veritable friendship quilt across the decades."

SPELLS FOR KEEPING A JOB

Once you have a job, conjure can help you to get promoted, be seen for the good work you do, and enhance your esteem among co-workers. It can give you courage to ask for and receive a pay raise, increased benefits, or vacation time. It can prevent layoffs, and help you keep the job you love.

SWEETENING YOUR CO-WORKERS

One of the best ways to gain favour at your work place is to have your co-workers and folks from other departments like you. An easy way to do this is to sweeten them. If your job site has a break room, grab a few sugar and sweetener packs and take them home. Layer them with sugar in a bowl and state your desire for sweet manners, respect, and cooperation. Leave the packets in your sugar bowl overnight. The next morning, taste some of your sugar and say, *"As sugar is sweet to me, so will my co-workers be sweet to me and show we favour."* Gently shake the packets off to remove the loose sugar. Take them back to your work place and add them back to the packets already there. Make sure you don't get caught. Every time your co-workers or bosses put sugar or sweeteners in their coffee or tea they will become more sweet to you.

You can make a regular habit of taking and replacing these packets. If your associates have business cards, put those in your sugar bowl at home; if not, write their names on slips of paper.

THE HIEROPHANTCARD TO FIX A BOSS FOR A RAISE

Here's a slick trick from Professor Porterfield's *"A Deck of Spells"*:

"To get an increase in your hours, a raise, extra overtime hours, or bonus money at the holidays, print out a copy of the Hierophant tarot card and write the name of your boss at the top of the card. Turn it over and write out a petition for your boss to quickly grant you your desired result. Take the card, turn it upside down and affix it to a purple glass-encased vigil candle. Dress the candle with a pinch of Ginger Root chips, Cinnamon chips, and nine drops of Boss Fix Oil. Place four half-dollar coins dressed with Fast Luck Oil around the candle in the shape of a cross. On a Thursday morning when the hands of the clock are rising, light the candle and pray the 108th Psalm over it each day that it continues burning."

OFFICE ALTAR FOR PROMOTION

From my book, *"Hoodoo Shrines and Altars"*:

A simple office altar can fit on the corner of your desk, in a desk drawer, or even into the frame of a picture to help keep it completely hidden. Some corporations have rules about what you can have on your desk, so adjust your altar to fit your corporate environment and its potential restrictions.

If you want to get promoted, whether there is a promotion available or not, build this altar in your office, on your desk, or in your work cubicle to help enhance your chances for success and recognition.

Start by writing out a petition for a promotion on a clean, square piece of paper. If possible, do this while on the job and at your desk, during a time that you will be free from interruption. Anoint a small lodestone with Crown of Success Oil and feed it a pinch of magnetic sand while stating your desire for a promotion.

Wrap your written petition tightly around the lodestone and place the wrapped lodestone in the bottom of a potted plant that can survive and thrive in an office environment. Try to avoid using a plant that requires a lot of sunlight if your office space doesn't get any sun. There are plenty of plants that are perfect for an office space; research what's best for your environment by asking someone at your local garden center. You may want to prepare two plants and keep one at home as a "spare" in case the first one shows stress from lack of light. Once your plant has been re-potted with the lodestone in the bottom, anoint the base of the pot with Crown of Success Oil.

Buy a simple desk toy. It can be a little squeezable stress ball or a wind-up walking robot, but the classic executive desk toy, known as "Balance Balls" or "Newton's Pendulum," is also highly suitable for this kind of an altar. Dress the desk toy with Crown of Success Oil, and as you do so, speak aloud your intention and desire for a promotion.

Place the dressed and loaded potted plant on your desk or in your cubicle along with the toy, which should be leaning against or touching the potted plant. Start your altar to work by encouraging your co-workers and boss to play with the little toy or to enjoy the flourishing plant at your desk. Let people pick up and play with the toy as often as they want to. This way you can offer it to your boss or co-workers when they are having a tough or stressful day. Every time they touch and use the toy they will be adding to your rise in the business, feeling gratitude towards you, and helping you to get one step closer to your desired promotion.

COMMANDING RESPECT AT THE WORKPLACE

Being respected and acknowledged for your skills in the workplace can really help you to feel happy in your job. When you aren't respected it can make work a miserable place to be. So let's get you some respect!

Wash your work clothes, using half a packet of Commanding Bath Crystals. Take a bath with the other half of the packet. Air dry and then put on your freshly-washed clothing.

With a needle, inscribe your name and the words *"Leadership and Respect"* into the wax of a 4-inch purple candle and dress it with Commanding Oil. Roll it in gold glitter and set it in a candle stand. Write out your petition, which should be a clear and concise explanation of your desires for control and respect. Sign your full name at the bottom of the paper and place it under the candle stand. Light some Commanding Incense and then light the candle. Speak your prayer out loud.

Repeat this process for seven days with seven candles. On the last day, while the final candle is burning, dress a High John the Conqueror Root, a silver dime, and a small lodestone with Commanding Oil. When the candle has finished, take your petition paper out from under it and crumple it around the curios that you have anointed. Tie this bundle up into a square of red flannel and carry it in your pocket.

SUCCESS AT A WORK MEETING

Gather together all of the paperwork that you will need to take with you to the meeting. Anoint a small purple candle with Commanding Oil. On a paper, cross the name of your boss with a brief command that you have for the meeting ahead. Place the paper under an overturned plate with the candle on top. Light the candle and complete the rest of this spell using only the light of the candle to see by.

Dress all of your papers with Commanding Sachet Powder. As you do this, concentrate on your power and how successful you will be. Recite Psalms 5 *("Give ear to my words, O Lord, consider my meditation")*. When you are finished working, snuff out the candle and go to bed.

In the morning before your meeting, light the candle and again recite Psalms 5. Anoint yourself with Commanding Oil and repeat your desire. Take out your petition paper and write Psalms 5 onto the paper. Put a pinch of sugar to sweeten your boss to you, fold the paper towards you, and put it in your shoe. If you can safely leave the candle burning, do so.

Spells for Getting a Loan

Getting a loan through a traditional bank requires specific qualifications. If your credit score is low you are unlikely to get a loan through a bank no matter how good your rootworking skills might be. Maipulating the luck of loans and credit successfully requires that you also take real world steps to clean up past financial messes and improve your standing. However, if you've got a few marks on your credit report, but mostly you are doing okay, conjure can help some of those blemishes not be seen. There are spells that you can do to hide certain things, have information get lost, or give you a lower interest rate when you might not normally qualify for one.

CONVINCING SOMEONE TO CO-SIGN FOR A LOAN

There are several ways to approach this spell. Your choice of which spiritual supply product to use will depend on the nature of the person you want to be your co-signer, and how pliable you think that person is.

You are going to dress a candle, and the oil you select will be based on the person whom you are approaching to co-sign the loan. If they are family members who are almost guaranteed to grant you this favour, use Blessing Oil. If they will agree once they hear you out, use Influence Oil. If they need just a little convincing, try Essence of Bend-Over Oil. If they look up to you as a leader, use Commanding Oil. If you think they really owe you this in return for your past favours to them, work with Compelling Oil. If they are stubborn or a tough to crack, or if they have already said no to similar requests, try to overpower them with Controlling Oil.

Using a needle, inscribe the potential co-signer's name into a 9-inch purple jumbo candle in a barber pole style spiral, and also inscribe the words *"Co-Sign My Loan"* in a barber pole spiral on the candle. Dress the candle with one or more of the above-listed oils and roll it in finely crushed Five Finger Grass. On either the person's photo or on a piece of paper torn from a brown paper bag, write the person's name nine times and then write directly on top of each line of their name write *"Co-Sign My Loan,"* also nine times. Place the photo or paper under the dressed and blessed candle and as you do so, state your petition out loud, light the candle, and recite the Lord's Prayer *("Our Father, who art in Heaven ...").* Let the candle burn all the way through and ask them to co-sign the loan.

A MOJO FOR GETTING A LOAN TO BUY SOMETHING

Cat Yronwode says, "Write your monetary petition *('Grant me the loan of $12,000.00')* or your affirmation *('The Bank of Umexa loans me $12,000.00')* or your prayer *('Dear Lord, Please sway the heart of Miss Sibley, the loan officer at the Bank of Umexa, that she may consent to loan me $12,000.00')* on a piece of paper and sign it with your name. On top of this, lay a small catalogue photo of whatever item you intend to purchase with the loan. On top of the photo place a pinch of Alfalfa leaves, a pinch of Five Finger Grass, and several whole Cloves. Wrap everything up into a packet and carry it in a green mojo bag dressed with Crown of Success Oil and Hoyt's Cologne when you go to the bank to ask for the loan."

DRESSING A ROOM FOR WRITING A LOAN APPLICATION

If you are filling out loan applications at home or in an office, always try to sit at the same desk or table. By locating yourself with respect to a particular chair, table, desk, or room as you engage in financial dealings, you can dress the space so that anything you do there will be set in your favour and support your mundane paperwork.

Start by blending Attraction Oil, Money Drawing Oil, and Five Finger Grass Oil. You can order these pre-mixed as a "Churches and Rootworkers Special" or blend a few drops of each as you pray over the mix. Dab a dot of oil in each corner of the room, on the floor, and in the center of the room. This creates a five-spot pattern that will mark your work space. Next, as applicable to your furnishings, mark each corner and the center of your desk, table, and chair, as well as the corners and back surface of your desktop or laptop computer. Finish by anointing the tips of all ten of your fingers, holding your hands in prayer, and reciting the 23rd Psalm *("The Lord is my shepherd, I shall not want ...")*. Your room is now prepared.

On a full sheet of letter paper, write out Psalms 112:5: *"A good man sheweth favour, and lendeth: he will guide his affairs with discretion"* followed directly by your petition, *"May my loan application be approved."* If you will be filling out handwritten paperwork, place this beneath the application forms. If you will be working at a computer, place it beneath the computer. However you turn in the application — by mail, in person, or electronically — keep a copy of your application with your petition-prayer paper. Light one 4-inch green candle dressed with the above oil blend on the papers daily for three days, or until the loan comes through.

LITTLE JOHN TO CHEW WHEN ASKING FOR A LOAN

While Harry Hyatt was in Brunswick, Georgia, in March 1939, he met a professional rootworker who was very articulate and told of having read books on occultism as well as collecting roots in the woods for use in magic. This man's name was lost by Hyatt, but he was recorded as Informant #1206. Among other things, he told Hyatt that Little John to Chew, also known as Low John, Court Case Root, Chew Root, or Galangal, is useful when borrowing money. He said, "Why, anywhere you want to borrow anything, why just go ahead and chew it and spit it around there and they'll take sides with you." However, he noted that the root would not work unless you left a silver dime as payment in the dirt where you dug it. He explained, "When you digging these roots and things, you should pay off in silver."

"Why is that?" asked Hyatt.

"Well, that's the sacrifice," said Informant #1206.

SKULL CANDLE FOR LOAN APPROVAL

Get a white skull candle and carve a hole in the bottom of the candle, big enough to load it with your petition paper. Keep all of the wax you've carved out, as you will need it later to seal the hole.

A skull candle is used to affect a specific person's mind, so you will need a personal link to the person who is handling your loan. A business card or a hand-written signature will suffice, or you may be able to print out the person's photo from a website. If nothing else, write the person's name on the printed logo of the institution that will be making the loan.

Put together a mix of Deer's Tongue leaf, Irish Moss, Alfalfa, and Five Finger Grass. On the business card or photo, write *"[Name], approve my loan"* three times. Cross their name with your own name, written nine times. Put the petition paper into the hole and seal it up with the wax that you had set aside. Carve *"[Name], approve my loan"* into the forehead area of the candle and dress the candle with Crown of Success Oil.

Light the candle, pray the 23rd Psalm, and whisper, *"[Name], you will grant the loan application from [Your Name]."* Speak your words kindly. Tell the skull that you are good for the loan. You will be a good risk. They want to approve you. Keep this stream of convincing whispered speech going for about ten minutes. Then snuff out the candle.

Repeat your prayer and whispered words for the next nine nights. On the last night, let the candle burn out and bury the remains in your backyard.

Spells for Getting a Settlement

Waiting for a settlement payment to come through can be a nerve-wracking experience. Mediation can be difficult enough, but if you have to go to court to get your money, the process can seem never-ending. The following spells are to help when dealing with insurance agents, government investigators, attorneys, and court judges.

SUBMITTING INSURANCE REIMBURSEMENT PAPERS

Back in March of 2010, a friendly member of the Lucky Mojo Forum who went by the pseudonym "Not Dorian Gray" posted some great tips for folks who are seeking insurance settlements. He wrote:

"I used to work in insurance claims, so I'll give you some practical pointers as well as magical work to do.

"First, *write your claim number on every page*. If you're faxing it, write it top and bottom, along with your last name in BLOCK CAPITALS. The number one reason that claims are delayed is that the claim number is incorrect or missing, and no one knows what the paperwork is actually for.

"Make sure you fax your claim to the right people. If it's a home insurance claim, don't fax it to the vehicle team by mistake. It'll get there eventually, probably … but it's always best to double check the fax number.

"Follow up the next day with a polite phone call to check that the paperwork arrived and is in order. No one is going to mind a quick phone call, and it will prompt them to look at the claim right then and there.

"Other things you can do:

"Make a little honey jar with your claim number and pop in some Compelling and Money Drawing condition oils and compelling herbs like Calamus and Licorice. Put the jar on top of the fax machine while you send your stuff through. This is also good for phones: I put my honey jar on the base of my cordless phone whenever I have to deal with the particular company I created it for. Since I started doing that, it's been easy going.

"If your claim is for house repair, make up a bath crystal solution with Money Drawing and Pay Me Crystals, put this in a spray bottle, and spray the damaged area of your home.

"Hope that helps you."

It does — and thank you, "Not Dorian Gray," whoever you are!

MEETING WITH YOUR BENEFITS CASEWORKER

Here is ConjureMan Ali's advice on how to prepare for an appointment with a caseworker who will determine if your benefits should continue:

"Make a name paper for the caseworker, dust it with Pay Me Powder, and place it in your left shoe. Sprinkle Compelling or Essence of Bend-Over Sachet Powder on your hand and brush it off. At the meeting, shake hands or touch the person and very quietly tap your foot as you speak to them. This will apply subtle pressure to them and get them to agree with you. When you get back home, call out the caseworker's name, command them to do what you want, and then stamp your foot hard on the name paper. The jolt is usually enough to get most people to do what you want.

"Carve the caseworker's name on a purple candle along with your command. Dress it with Compelling and Pay Me Oils, burn it on their picture or name paper while praying Psalms 114 (*'When Israel went out of Egypt ...'*) and Psalms 110 (*'The Lord said unto my Lord ...'*), and then calling out your command. Burn Calamus on charcoal with the incense of your choice while speaking to the spirit of the Calamus to go and grab hold of the senses of your target and make them bend to your will.

"The trick to influencing people is knowing how to get at them. Some people are best influenced and controlled through pressure, others become meek to a seemingly iron will, while others must be knocked off balance to influence their mind. Hit your caseworker from different angles."

LITTLE JOHN TO CHEW FOR COURT CASE VICTORY

Before going into court, place a small piece of Little John to Chew Root in your mouth. It is very hot and spicy; don't use too much. While in court, well before the judge makes a decision, spit on the floor of the courtroom. This may not be easily done, so be sure that you do so undetected.

TWO SIMPLE COURT CASE SHOE SPELLS

• To sweeten a judge, take a small amount of sweet jam or jelly and smear it on a name paper of the judge who will be hearing your case. Fold the paper closed. On the day of court, wear that paper in your shoe.

• On one piece of paper write the names of the Apostles and on a second paper write Psalms 34:14 (*"Depart from evil, and do good; seek peace, and pursue it."*). Wear one paper in your right shoe and the other in your left shoe. This will help all concerned to be fair-minded in court.

PSALMS 37 IF FALSE CLAIMS ARE MADE AGAINST YOU

Psalms 37 (*"Fret not thyself because of evildoers ..."*) is useful in cases where a malicious accuser or tale-bearer may make trouble for you. Light a brown candle dressed with Stop Gossip Oil and, as it burns, wash with Stop Gossip Bath Crystals in water to cleanse away false accusations that have been spoken or written. Recite Psalms 37 while you are in the bath.

SPEED UP THE JUDGEMENT IN AN INJURY LAWSUIT

ConjureMan Ali does a lot of court case work for his clients, and here is his advice on how to speed up a lagging insurance claim:

"Court Case work is definitely needed if mediation has failed and your injury claim is going before a judge. Burn brown candles dressed with Court Case Oil while praying your desire for justice and for a speedy conclusion that favours you. Psalms 35 (*"Plead my cause, O Lord ..."*) is great for invoking divine aid, and Psalms 37 (*"Fret not thyself because of evildoers ..."*) does away with the opposition's attempts to besmirch you.

"Dress all your papers with Court Case Sachet Powders and if you have to make an appearance in court, either create a mojo hand with Little John to Chew Root or prepare to actually chew the root and spit it in court.

Deer's Tongue herb can help bolster the eloquence and persuasiveness of your attorney. You can create a honey jar for him as well to help him favour you more. Attorneys are often very busy and a honey jar can influence him to put in a bit of extra work to get things done faster.

"In addition, I would burn Road Opener candles to help clear out any bureaucratic blocks and help the paperwork get cleared up. If you are comfortable working with Catholic saints, Saint Expedite is a helpful spirit who can be petitioned to expedite the process if it is still dragging on.

"Finally, a vinegar jar containing the names of the opposition's lawyers will make them seem sour and unattractive to the judge."

Miss Cat adds a few more tips for this kind of situation:

"If you are working a Court Case spell to get a monetary settlement, add Pay Me spiritual supplies to your Court Case spiritual supplies. Be sure to specify who is to do the paying, if you add their names to a honey jar.

"If you have an ongoing disability claim filed with a state caseworker, add Five Finger Grass to your honey jar, so that favours will be granted.

"If the amount of investigatory work being conducted against you seems intrusive, burn a few Stop Gossip or Law Keep Away Candles."

A HONEY JAR FOR A COURT SETTLEMENT

If you've made a love honey or sugar jar, you'll be able to handle a court case jar for a financial settlement. The major differences between them are the herbs and oils that are used, and the colour of the candles.

First, your petition may require some consideration. If monetary negotiations have already failed and you are in small claims court or at trial, sweetness has already frayed thin. So who do you really want to sweeten? Is it the judge, an attorney, or a jury? Who needs to be most influenced in the situation? Your answer might be, "All of the above," in which case you can make a separate packet for each party and place them all in one jar. You won't be able to get personal effects, but do try to find photos online, or signatures on court documents.

Select herbs to fold into the name-packets from the list on page 15, but be sure that anything you put into honey or sugar is edible, for as the court date approaches, you can benefit from eating some of the sweetener.

Set brown candles dressed with Court Case and Pay Me Oils on your jar.

A HONEY JAR TO GET CHILD SUPPORT

Often child support spells are undertaken with aggression and a desire to control what remains of a failed romance. However, sometimes a sweet approach can actually work better because it encourages the support-paying parent to not only contribute, but also to be involved in the child's life.

Create a honey jar that includes personal effects from all members of the family — you, the child or children, and the other parent. If you have a photo of all of you together, use the back of that for your petition paper. Write out both parents' names side-by-side nine times, forming two columns. Cross this with the child's name written at right angles over the top of those two, as the child is what holds this relationship together. If there are several children, write each one's name three times. Encircle the names with the phrase, *"We are a family forever"* repeated over and over.

Draw hearts in each corner of the petition paper with a dollar sign in the center of each heart. Under each heart write the words *"Pay child support."* Put a pinch of Rosemary, which gives women power, into the paper, and add a pinch each of Calendula, Deer's Tongue, and Little John to Chew. Fold the paper toward you and put it in the jar. Burn alternating green and pink candles dressed with Pay Me Oil on the jar. Keep this honey jar working as needed, until your child turns eighteen.

Spells for Success in Business

Starting a business can be an exciting new adventure and also a scary financial investment. Whether it's an online shop, a consultancy, a brick and mortar store, or a home business, you will need money for everything from inventory, rent, utilities, advertising, shipping, and travel to uniforms, licenses, business cards, office supplies, and taxes. It takes money-luck to make money in business, and these spells can help.

A WORKING MONEY ALTAR FOR YOUR SHOP

This altar invites wealth, so give it the space that you want wealth to take up in your business. The top of a display cabinet would work — or take a cue from the wall altars you may have seen in Asian restaurants: right in sight of all the customers, they definitely attract attention.

Start by cleansing the space and sprinkling it with Wealthy Way Sachet Powder. In the center, put a statue that symbolizes wealth to you. It may be Hotei Buddha, a Beckoning Cat, Saint Martin Caballero, the Seven Lucky Gods, Lord Kubera, Goddess Lakshmi, a Lucky Pig, Saint Expedite, Nang Kwak, Kuan Kung, Caishen, Saint Lazarus, or a trunk-up Elephant. Whoever it is — and you can have more than one — the statue should be beautiful and make you happy when you see it. Your customers will ask questions about it, so be prepared to tell the story! It doesn't need to be a huge piece, but it should be at least six inches tall.

Write a paper with your name on it seven times, encircled by the word *"wealth"* written over and over without lifting your pen off the paper. Fold it three times toward yourself and place it under the statue. Dress and bless a two-dollar bill and lay it in front of the statue. On top of this set a small bowl containing items that represent wealth to you. They can be charms, curios, coins, stones, or tokens. Keep adding items to this bowl as lucky trinkets come your way. To each side of the statue have a green candle dressed in Wealthy Way Oil. Burn these candles any time you have to make a big financial decision, need more income, or require financial support.

If this altar is at the right height, your customers will begin to leave their spare change and paper currency all over it. Donate the money to charity or use it to make up what is lacking when customers can't quite find enough in their pockets to make a purchase.

MONEY-T FOR PROSPERITY AND BUSINESS SUCCESS

This recipe comes from *"Hoodoo Spiritual Baths"* by Aura Laforest:

"Make an herbal blend consisting of 1/2 cup Yellow Dock root, 3/4 cup Sassafras root, 1 stick Cinnamon, 3 teaspoons whole Cloves, and 1 teaspoon Allspice berries. Cut or crush the larger items to a uniform texture, so you can measure the mixture out. On a Thursday or Friday, as the clock hands rise, or before sunrise, prepare 3 tablespoons of the herbs in 3 cups of spring water. Simmer on the stove-top, covered, for 21 minutes and strain. Bathe in this and pray Psalms 23 *("The Lord is my shepherd ...")*. Keep a cup of the used bath water that now has your essence in it and add that water to the scrub water for business when you clean the floors."

TEN OF CLUBS MIXTURE FOR A SUCCESSFUL BUSINESS

This comes from Professor Charles Porterfield's *"A Deck of Spells"*:

"To draw customers to an established business, first take the Ten of Clubs and write the success sigil "$$¢¢$$" at the top, middle, and foot of the card. Next burn the Ten of Clubs to ash, reciting the 114th Psalm *('When Isræl went out of Egypt ...')* over the card as it burns. Collect the ashes from the card and mix them with a packet of Money Drawing Incense Powder and equal parts powdered Irish Moss and Earth Smoke. Divide the mixture in half, then sprinkle half of the mixture around the front door of the business and outside along the sidewalk in front of the business. Burn the second part of the mixture over live charcoal in the mornings before opening up the business, reciting the 108th Psalm *('O God, my heart is fixed ...')* aloud as you fumigate inside the store with the smoke from the burning mixture."

In my experience, once you have prepared and prayed over Professor Porterfield's Ten of Clubs Mixture, you will find additional uses for it:

Include it as an ingredient in mojo bags by adding a pinch or two to any money hand along with the other roots, minerals, herbs, and curios.

Add it to a bottle of Money Drawing Oil, along with a few grains of Frankincense, to give the oil a bit of an added boost.

Ground to a fine powder with a coffee-grinder or in mortar, it can be mixed with your foot-track dirt and deployed for wealth around your shop.

The powder can also be mixed half-and-half with Frankincense and Dragon's Blood and used as a resin incense to burn over charcoal.

Finally, it can be used to dust or double-dress anointed candles that have been fixed with Prosperity Oil for better business success.

EIGHT QUICK TRICKS FOR BRICK AND MORTAR SHOPS

These simple shopkeepers' tricks keep your prosperity coming in:

- Brew a tea of Cinnamon, Sassafras, Calendula, and sugar, then prinkle or sweep it from the street curb or parking area toward your front door.
- Sprinkle Money Drawing Sachet Power under the entry mat.
- Sprinkle Irish Moss, Cinnamon powder, and sugar under the entry mat.
- Dress products near the front door with Look Me Over Oil or Powder.
- Dust your business cards with Look Me Over, Attraction, and Money Drawing Sachet Powders. Set them where customers can take one.
- Lift the wooden threshold "saddle" at the front door, nail four heads-up Indian Head pennies under it for protection, and replace it.
- If you are bothered by unruly customers, sprinkle Black Snake Root and Boldo herb under the door mat to keep them away.
- If you are bothered by the police, fire marshals, or health inspectors, lay a line of red brick dust under the mat across the entrance door as you pray Psalms 91 *("He that dwelleth in the secret place ...")*.

CUT A PENNY IN TWO FOR BUSINESS LUCK

In February 1939, Informant #995 in Saint Petersburg. Florida, told Harry Hyatt how to have luck in business: "You take a penny and cut that penny half in two, if you want to be lucky with money. You put one half in your left pocket and leave the other half home, and you're going to be lucky in getting money in any kind of business you go into. That's luck. I've tested that out. That's extreme luck."

LODESTONE NEST FOR A BRICK AND MORTAR SHOP

Prepare a money-drawing lodestone as described on page 36, and set it in a little nest with a folded two-dollar bill and coins of every denomination in your cash register. Be sure to include one coin from the nest — your trained hunting money — in the change you give to your first customer of the day. Replace the coin with another to keep the lodestone working.

ANNUAL BRICK AND MORTAR SHOP CLEANING

Once a year, raise your shop's energy with a thorough spiritual cleaning. Wash with hot water and Chinese Wash, from top to bottom and back to front. Seal each room with a prayer and light a white candle as you finish it.

THREE SIDEWALK WASHES FOR MAIN STREET SHOPS

These come to us from Miss Cat's *"Hoodoo Herb and Root Magic"*:

- **New-Business Sidewalk Wash:** When starting a new business, first wash outward with a tablespoonful of ammonia and a tablespoonful of Chinese Wash in a bucket of water to clear out bad influences. Then mix Cinnamon and sugar into water and wash inward to draw in customers.
- **Sidewalk Wash To Draw Money to a Business:** Early in the morning, mix a tablespoonful of powdered Allspice, a teaspoonful of saltpeter, and half a cup of sugar into a bucket of water. Mop with this from the sidewalk toward the door, then in the door, through the store, and all the way to the back of the building.
- **Once-A-Week Business-Drawing Sidewalk Wash:** Mix Cinnamon, sugar, and your own first urine of the day (collected before speaking to anyone) in a bucket of scrub water and wet-sweep the sidewalk toward the door, to draw in customers. Alternatively, mix Cinnamon Oil with the sugar and substitute ammonia for the urine, or just use sugar and Fast Luck Oil, which contains Cinnamon Oil, to make up the wash.

WHITE CANDLE AND YELLOW CANDLE

In 1938 in Memphis, Tennessee, Informant #947, a wise business owner, shared these traditional shopkeeper's candle tricks with Rev. Hyatt:

"You burn your white candle for money when you first going into business, and you use chamber lye, a little your chamber lye and sugar for to draw your trade. You takes and mops with it, see. Mop your floor right good with a little chamber lye and sugar.

"When you bidding [inviting] customers, you should burn success incense and use yellow candles. Burn a yellow candle in the morning, soon in the morning, around five or six o'clock in the morning. You burn it up; that's to make you have success."

BUSINESS RECOVERY AFTER A BAD WEEK

Light Money Drawing Incense on arriving at the shop. Step over the burning incense three times, fully smoking yourself. In a wash bucket, add the incense ashes, your urine, sugar, Cinnamon, Money Drawing Oil, and Van Van Bath Crystals. Wash the space, top to bottom and back to front. Praying for losses to be gone, sweep back toward the door for new trade.

14-DAY MONEY-DRAWING SPELL FOR A BUSINESS

From *"Hoodoo in Theory and Practice"* by Catherine Yronwode:

"You will need seven green 4-inch candles, Irish Moss, magnetic sand, a large lodestone, a bottle of Money Drawing Oil, Money Drawing Sachet Powder, seven two-dollar bills, and seven silver dimes.

Begin on a new Moon. Place the lodestone on a tray where it can stay for the duration of the work. Dress all of the candles with Money Drawing Oil and arrange them in a crescent around the back of the lodestone. Every morning, starting from the left, pick up one of the green candles and anoint it again with Money Drawing Oil and light it. Anoint four corners of one of the two-dollar bills with Money Drawing Oil and place that bill under the lodestone. As you do this, recite the 23rd Psalm or a simple wish, such as *'May my money increase.'* Feed the lodestone with magnetic sand and say, *'Lodestone, as you draw these sands to you, draw money to me by day.'* Let the candle burn half way and pinch out the flame. By the end of seven days all of the candles will be half-burned.

"Now switch to doing the work for seven nights. Re-anoint a green candle with Money Drawing Oil and re-light it, but this time anoint a coin with Money Drawing Oil and place it with the lodestone as you say the Psalm or your wish — and when you feed the lodestone, say, *'Lodestone, as you draw these sands to you, draw money to me by night.'* Each night let one candle burn out, until they are all out. The spell ends at the Full Moon.

Clear the table and bury any candle wax left over at a crossroads. If you worked the spell at home, take the tray with the lodestone, the magnetic sand, and the money to your place of business. Now, at the business site, sprinkle or blow Money Drawing Sachet Powder in the four corners of the room. Place a pinch of Irish Moss in the center of the room.

Take the bills and coins off the tray and put them in your cash register. Place the lodestone with its magnetic sand either in the cash register or near it, out of sight. The lodestone will draw money to your place of business as long as you feed it once a week with magnetic sand and also allow it to physically touch some incoming money at least once a week to keep it trained to draw money. Give the dressed money out in change to customers; it will go into the world and bring more money back to your place of business to be with the lodestone.

Renew the Money Drawing Sachet Powder and the Irish Moss after every cleaning of the room that would remove them.

MONEY MASTER JAR FOR A BUSINESS

Cleanse a Mason jar by swirling Florida Water inside and pouring it out. When the jar is dry, add Bayberry, Five Finger Grass, Cinnamon, Solomon Seal Root, Master of the Woods, Master Root, and a lodestone. Prepare an Alligator foot by placing a Mercury dime in it, and using green thread to wrap the paw and hold the coin in place. Tie the string off with three knots. Set the Alligator foot in the jar. Sprinkle magnetic sand over the items and feed the jar a drop of whiskey. Cap the jar and hide it near the front door of your business. Feed it a drop of whiskey daily.

MOVING MERCHANDISE

Every item you sell can be fixed to draw a paying customer. Depending on what they are made of, you can dress, dust, or smoke them with Look Me Over and Attraction Oils, Powders, or Incense. Do this both to new inventory and to unsold goods that are going on markdown sale.

DRESS A PHOTOGRAPH FOR SELLING ONLINE

If you sell at an online site, you want your merchandise to get noticed. Print out a photo of each item that you have listed online. At the center of the image, write the dollar amount you want to sell the item for. Anoint the four corners and the center of the photo with Look Me Over Oil. Circle the image with the word *"sell"* written over and over again, without lifting your pen from the paper. Set a green glass-encased candle dressed with Crown of Success, Money Drawing, and Pay Me Oils on the photo and keep it burning as long as the item is for sale. If you list many items, print them out, dress each photo and put them in a keepsake box with the candle on top so that your online sales grow and increase.

DRESS YOURSELF FOR HIGH COMMISSIONS

If you sell on commission, you know that you have to make a good impression on your customers. Every morning before heading off to work dress yourself with Prosperity Oil. Wear it alone or add a couple of drops of it to Hoyt's cologne or your favourite perfume or aftershave. Put it on your wrists, behind your ears, and behind your knees. As you anoint yourself recite the Lord's Prayer or Psalms 23, followed by your goal or wish, something like: *"I will reach and exceed my sales goals. I will attract eager customers with money to spend. I am successful."*

Spells for Gambling Luck

Playing games of chance is fun, but winning games of chance is a whole lot better. From casino slots and keno, to poker or dice with friends, all the way to racetrack bets and hitting the numbers in the lottery, there are lots of ways to gamble and almost as many ways to help yourself with conjure.

DRESSING YOURSELF FOR GAMBLING LUCK

Check over the lucky gambling formulas on page 17, and select one or more to work with. Before going out to gamble, smoke yourself and your clothing with a lucky incense as you recite the 23rd Psalm. Dust your hands with a lucky sachet powder, as you pray to win. Dress yourself with a lucky oil on your wrists, behind your earlobes, and behind your knees.

PROTECT YOUR HAIR

Your hair is lucky and people are known to touch a winner's hair to drain their luck. Don't let it happen to you. At the casinos, dress your hair with Protection Oil or I Can You Can't Oil, and wear a wig, if necessary.

SIX SIMPLE GAMBLER'S TRICKS

Here are six quick spells to dress and bless yourself for gambling:

- **Wear Hoyt's Cologne for Luck:** Dress your hands, your hair, the soles of your feet, and the coins in your pocket with Hoyt's Cologne.
- **Sleep on a Dream Book:** If you are having a hard time catching lucky numbers, sleep with a dream book under your pillow and dream lucky.
- **Powder Your Cards:** When playing cards with friends, if you are able to use your own deck, lay your cards on a flat surface, put a pinch of Three Jacks and a King Powder in your hand, and blow it on the cards.
- **Incubate Your Lottery Tickets:** While waiting for the numbers, set your tickets under a candle fixed with Lucky Number or Lucky 13 Oil.
- **Dress Your Pocket Change:** Lightly dress your pocket change with lucky oils. If playing a slot machine, use Pay Me Oil so it will pay out.
- **Drink Lucky Tea:** Brew a tea with the lucky herbs on page 17, being careful to select only non-toxic ones. Pray over it, strain it, sweeten to taste, and put it in a water bottle to sip from at the races or at play.

USE COMFREY TO PREPARE CURRENCY FOR GAMBLING

Miss Cat says, "Dress a fresh Comfrey leaf with Money Drawing Oil and wrap it around your money, folding the leaf toward you. Keep the money this way overnight, or, better yet, for three days, or until the day you take it out to gamble. Use dried Comfrey leaves the same way, or keep them in your wallet with your money."

HIRE YOUR LUCK OUT

When going out to gamble or play games of chance, hire a rootworker to burn lucky candles on your behalf to help hold your luck. Of course, you can burn these candles on your own, but candle safety is highly important! If you can't be sure that your candles will be safe burning at home while you are away, don't risk it! Having a rootworker hold vigil for you can add extra luck while you are at the tables or playing the machines. It's like a battery, keeping your luck magic going.

LUCKY STONE GAMBLING MOJO

Lucky stones, also called fishhead rocks, lucky bones, or lucky rocks, are the otoliths or ear bones of Drumfish, Drumhead, Sheephead, Croaker, Gaspergou, Puppy Drum, Redfish, and other species common throughout the South, East, Midwest, and Canada. The paired, disc-shaped ear bones at the back of the Drumfish's skull are sought after for gambling and business luck. The fish's right-side bone is naturally marked with an "L" shape and its left-side bone is marked with a "J" shape. Some say these marks stand for Lord Jesus. Others say they mean Luck and Joy or Love and Joy.

There are various regional traditions for the use of lucky stones, but this mojo will get you started. It is the kind made by Miss Cat for her clients, and she explains that it is "based on a gambler's hand that Rev. Harry Hyatt learned about back in 1938, from Informant #958, a professional rootworker in Memphis, Tennessee."

"Cut out two small, circular disks of chamois leather and whip-stitch them together half-way. Sandwich a silver dime between a pair of lucky fishhead rocks, filling in and surrounding them with softened Lakshmi Dhoop incense into which you have embedded Grains of Paradise. Whip-stitch the mojo tight and dress the leather cover with Double Luck Perfume Oil. Keep it oiled and fed, and wear it in your pocket for gambling luck."

SIX GAMBLING HANDS FROM CAT YRONWODE

These lucky mojos come to us from *"Hoodoo Herb and Root Magic"*:

BLACK CAT MOJO FOR GAMBLING LUCK

"Black Cat hair is said to bring powerful luck when mixed with Patchouli and Tobacco in a mojo hand or added with them to Black Cat Oil. Folks also use this oil to anoint a Black Cat candle, which they burn while dressing the money they will use to buy lottery tickets."

LUCKY DICE CRAP-SHOOTERS' MOJO

"A fine gambling hand is made with a pair of lucky dice that have been 'retired' from play, and a pinch each of Five Finger Grass, Cinnamon, Irish Moss, Thyme, and Cloves in a red flannel bag. Dress the bag with Lady Luck Oil, Special Dice Oil, or Hoyt's Cologne."

BLUEING, ALUM, AND SILVER GAMBLING MOJO

"A blueing ball, a lump of rock alum, and nine silver dimes sewn up together in a red flannel bag is a good gaming charm."

OLD-TIME HOYT'S COLOGNE GAMBLING HAND

"Get a piece of Ginseng root, a piece of Black Snake Root, a High John the Conqueror Root, and three fresh seeds from a green (unripe) Red Pepper. Fold these toward you into a scrap of red flannel, soak it overnight in Hoyt's Cologne, sew it up very tight, and carry it in a red flannel bag."

CARD-PLAYERS' LUCKY GAMBLING HAND

"Combine Five Finger Grass with Lucky Hand Root and an Alligator foot to aid in 'all the skills that five fingers can perform.' Carry this hand in a red flannel bag dressed with Three Jacks And A King Oil and fed with Hoyt's Cologne while at play."

A RABBIT FOOT MOJO FOR GAMBLING LUCK

"A traditional conjure hand for playing games of chance contains a silver dime, a Rabbit foot, and nine short lengths of Devil's Shoe Strings which have been tightly rolled up and tied inside a dollar bill on which you have written your name. The three ingredients are carried in a red flannel bag dressed with the urine or menstrual blood of the gambler's beloved."

MY OWN FAVOURITE GAMBLING MOJO

Burn Gambler's Gold herbs on charcoal as you put a Lucky Hand Root, a High John the Conqueror Root, a Mercury dime, a whole Nutmeg, and a pinch each of Five Finger Grass and Cinnamon Chips in a green bag. Make a name paper and all over it write words like *"winner," "big money," "jackpot,"* and *"beat the house."* Put the paper in the bag, whisper your wish, and tie the string. Feed it whiskey and Lucky Mojo Oil, and smoke it.

"GRAINS O' PAIR O' DICE" TO CHEW

Miss Cat says, "Gamblers keep a handful of Grains of Paradise in a pocket and chew them while at play, spitting surreptitiously onto their hands to dress them before throwing their dice. Grains of Paradise can also be added to any mojo hand carried for good luck."

LUCKY RABBIT'S FOOT AND VAN VAN OIL

Dress a Rabbit's foot with Van Van Oil. Wear it in your pocket and rub the foot before stepping up to a new game or slot machine. When you are on a winning streak, grab the foot and share some of that luck with it.

PAY THIRTY PENNIES FOR A BEGGAR'S DIRT

In 1939, when Rev. Hyatt was in Sumter, South Carolina, he met "The Courtroom Specialist," a middle-aged rootworker. This is his gambling hand: "Pay 30 pennies for dirt from a beggar's grave, head, chest, and foot. Buy a packet of needles and wrap three of them, two long and one short, with red thread into a cross shape. Sew the needles and a pinch of dirt in chamois." He made and sold these mojos for 50 cents each, back in the day.

LUCK AND WISDOM IN THE STOCK MARKET

It takes luck as well as wisdom to make money from the stock market.

For lucky stock picks from dreams, dress your forehead with Aunt Sally's Lucky Dream Oil before going to bed, and keep a note pad by your bed to write down what comes to mind when you wake up.

For wise stock choices, and for timing issues, anoint your forehead with King Solomon Wisdom Oil as you read the daily business news.

Dress a green vigil light with Prosperity Oil. Use a marker to write the names of your stocks on the glass. Write the success sigil ($$¢¢$$) around the bottom in an unbroken band. Let the candle burn straight through.

A SPIRITUAL MINISTER AND A WHOREHOUSE MADAME

Here's a chance to get to know a couple of Harry Hyatt's informants. Each contributor was unique, as you can see from their backgrounds.

DOCTOR SIMS' GRAINS OF PARADISE GAMBLING HAND

In 1937, Rev. Hyatt met Doctor Sims, a conjure professional from New Orleans who was working in the District of Columbia at the time. A Spiritual Church minister, he taught his pupils to study the Bible. When they passed their exams, he got them certificates of ordination from Saint John's Temple, an institution which he said had more White members than Black ones. He explained his gambling hand to Hyatt as a fellow academic might:

"In gambling, we say you can take a little piece of High John the Conker, you take three Guinea Grain seeds, you take a piece of lodestone, you take magic sand, and you sew these in a piece of cloth. Upon your hands you would use Oil of Van Van. Then you would hold this lucky charm in your hand whilst you are playing with a piece of money and you will be lucky."

"What is magic sand?" asked Hyatt.

"Magic sand is a thing that is made to go with this lodestone. It looks like black dust, but it comes with lodestone. You buy lodestone and they give you this sand with it," said Doctor Sims, perfectly describing magnetic sand.

PAINT A SILVER DOLLAR WITH MENSTRUAL BLOOD

Hyatt called Informant #1545, whom he met in Memphis, Tennessee, in 1939, "a first-class hoodoo doctor; a person free from routine and sensitive to changing social conditions." She had children and she owned a brothel: "I got a house I runs, peoples in there, girls hustling, you understand, and I does what I can for luck and peace." She described a unique money charm that a man such as Mr. Hyatt could have his wife make for him:

"Well, I hate to tell that." (She was reluctant to discuss Mrs. Hyatt's menstruation.) "You know, just like you got a wife or lady, or something. You carry a fifty-cent piece to her or a silver dollar, and let her take some of her ministrate and paint that over twice, just like paint, you see, just on top, on half of it. Then turn it over and paint another half, a two-corner, on opposite halves of the dollar. And so let it dry. Paint it over twice, you know — twice good, you know, where it'll have a good coat. And you can put it in your pocket with all kinds of money, and go in any kind of gambling game and won't never lose no money."

GAMBLER'S LUCKY WASH AND CARD BLESSING

This lucky wash is old school and traditional. Harry Hyatt picked it up from Informant #959 on his first trip to Memphis, Tennessee, in 1938. Mix a crushed blueing ball or Reckitt's Crown Blue square with equal parts saltpeter and sugar, and keep this in a sealed jar. Before you go out to play cards, dissolve a small amount of the mix into water, add your own urine, bathe downward, and say the Lord's Prayer three times to cleanse yourself. After this, dress the edges of your playing cards with "any kind of lucky oil that you believe in" to draw a win. When Hyatt asked this worker for a personal favourite lucky oil, the reply was "Rose Oil from the drugstore."

GUNPOWDER AND GRAINS OF PARADISE MOJO

On Hyatt's second trip to Memphis, Tennessee, in 1939, he met Informant #1541 and got this mojo recipe: "Well, you take gunpowder and lodestone and nine seeds of Red Pepper, and sew it up in a rag. That's for to draw luck to you, for money. You know, if you's a gambler, why, you can win, and if you're a policy player, why, you win like that. Or if you a business man, why, you know, your business will be more urgent [livelier]."

SAINT EXPEDITE AND A GAMBLING HAND

In 1940 in Algiers, Louisiana, Informant #1577 — the same Catholic worker who told how to call on Saint Anthony for help in poverty — gave Rev. Hyatt a tip about petitioning Saint Expedite for gambling luck. Like many residents of that region, she called him "Saint Espidee." Although his usual colour is red, she explained that when you want gambling help from him, you make green offerings, to bring in the greenbacks.

"Saint Espidee is for gamblers. You gives him anything green; a candle or flowers or a green vegetable, for money. He's for gamblers. You prays when you go to him and you'd ask him, say, *'Saint Espidee, I want you to help me to get some money. I'm goin' out and gamble and if I be successful and get this money, I will give you a bunch of flowers. Or give you so much of something green. I'll take the money and buy it and give it to you.'* When you gets this money, you go to some church, or if you got him in your house, you buys the stuff and you puts it in front of him for a sacrifice."

She also shared her favourite gambling hand: Black Snake Root, Devil's Shoe String, John the Conqueror Root, Cinnamon, and a silver dime, sewn in chamois leather and dressed with Van Van Oil.

AN ALLIGATOR FOOT IS LUCKY

Miss Cat says, "An Alligator foot may be used as a lucky key-chain fob or pocket piece and fed with whiskey, urine, Hoyt's Cologne, or Van Van Oil to get it working. It is also a strong ingredient in a lucky hand, and may be combined with two or more curios, such as a whole Nutmeg, Allspice berries, Cinnamon, Bayberry, or a High John the Conqueror Root. If setting it on an altar, write your money wishes written in red ink on a two-dollar bill, jam it in between the claws, and secure it with glue."

LADY LUCK OVERNIGHT GAMBLING TRIP SPELL

Ladies, prepare yourself for winning before you head to the casinos! Start while the Moon is waxing, or when the Moon is in Gemini, or on a Wednesday. You'll need seven days to work before you leave on your trip.

On day one, get up before dawn and bathe with Lady Luck Bath Crystals. Recite the 23rd Psalm, pour the bath water over your head. and keep a cup of the bath water. Carry it to a crossroads, throw it eastward, and walk home.

Back home, light Lady Luck Incense and mark a green jumbo candle to divide it into seven parts. Carve your name in the wax, and double-dress the candle with Lady Luck Oil and Lady Luck Sachet Powders. Write your petition: *"On my trip to [Place] with the help of God, I will win big and more than cover all of my expenses."* Sign it with your name, put it under the candle, and light the candle. Let it burn to the first mark, then snuff it out.

Bathe, light incense, and burn the candle every morning. On day seven, take the last bath and let the candle burn out. Dress your clothes with Lady Luck Sachet Powder and pack some Lady Luck supplies for use when you arrive. Wrap the spell remains in cloth and bury them in your backyard.

When you get to your hotel room, blow Lady Luck Sachet Powder into each corner, as you recite the 23rd Psalm. Before heading out to play, wash your face and hands with Lady Luck Bath Crystals. Anoint your fingers and pulse points with Lady Luck Oil — and you are ready to win!

PAYING THE SPIRIT OF A WINNING GAMBLER

When Rev. Hyatt was in Brunswick, Georgia, in 1939, Informant #1186 told him that to win at poker, you go at midnight to the grave of a gambler, open a small hole, take out a pinch of dirt, and pay the spirit in advance by filling the hole with coins, then closing it back up. Wrap the dirt in a small piece of cloth and place it where you keep your money when you go to play.

Spells for Money from the Streets

When making money from illegal activities, you want to attract business success while keeping safe from law enforcement. This is tricky because you are calling in customers, but blocking specific kinds of attention.

LAW KEEP AWAY SPRINKLE FOR AN ILLEGAL BUSINESS
From Professor Charles Porterfield's *"The Sporting Life"*:
"Powder together Dragon's Blood resin, Flax seed, Camphor, salt, manure from a white Horse, and dirt from the foot of a grave; sprinkle this around the building, at the threshold, or in the yard to keep the police away. This sprinkle may also be used on goods that are to be kept hidden at a location away from your home or place of business."

TWO-WAY FLOOR SCRUB FOR TRADE IN ILLEGAL GOODS
This recipe is from Cat Yronwode, who says she used it herself, back in the day. "Here's how to keep off the law while attracting trade to your location. Combine one tablespoonful each of oil of Bergamot, oil of Cloves, and oil of Cedar in a bucket of water. Write the name of the Captain of Police on paper, burn the paper to ashes, add the ashes to your scrub water, and scrub the place outward toward the front door and onto the sidewalk to drive off intruders. Then make up a second wash with one tablespoonful each of oil of Cinnamon, your own urine, and sugar in a second bucket of water. Scrub back from the sidewalk into the building to draw in customers."

PINS AND NEEDLES TO KEEP OFF THE LAW
In 1939, in Waycross, Georgia, Rev. Hyatt met Informant #1110, a man engaged in "runnin' a bad house." He advised to "Get a new pincushion and two packs of needles. Stick the needles in everywhere, and hang it over the door. You won't get pulled in; but if you are, you'll get clear."

DRESSING A GENITAL CANDLE FOR CASH TIPS
Load a pink or red genital candle with your pubic, body, or head hairs, seal it up, and dress it with either Follow Me Boy or Follow Me Girl Oil, to suit your client base. Set it on a plate with coins and currency all around it, then burn it 15 minutes at a time, twice a day, morning and night.

DOUBLE LUCK PERFUME OIL FOR SEX AND CASH

Double Luck Perfume Oil contains two liquids — green for money and red for passion. If you mix up your cash and your sex, shake it up before using! Wear Double Luck Perfume when you go to work. Depending on how you present yourself, add to it a few drops of Follow Me Boy, Follow Me Girl, Jezebel, Essence of Bend-Over, or Cleo May Oil, as desired.

A LODESTONE UNDER THE BED

On the evening of the full Moon, well before sunset, write your name on a paper nine times and circle it with a wish like: *"May well-paying, safe customers come to me."* Lay it on a plate, cover it with a two-dollar bill, and set a lodestone on top. Bathe with Look Me Over Bath Crystals, collect a cup of your bath water, and carry it to a crossroads. If you timed yourself right, the Moon will be rising as you get there. Throw the water toward the Moon and say, *"As the Moon rises, may this month bring me profit and pleasure."* Walk home and don't look back. Once home, dress the lodestone with Money Drawing Oil, feed it with magnetic sand, and say, *"As I feed you, so you will feed me."* Cover the plate with an overturned bowl to keep dust off, and hide it under your bed. To prepare your room for visitors, blow a mix of Jezebel and Cleo May Sachet Powder onto the bed sheets and dress the four corners of the bedstead with a blend of Jezebel and Cleo May Oil.

THREE QUICK SEX WORKER'S TIPS

- If you work by phone or camera, dress your equipment prior to using it by smoking it lightly in Look Me Over Incense.
- If you go out to meet customers, dust your shoes with Look Me Over, Cleo May, and Money Drawing Powders before leaving the house.
- If your work takes place in a specific room, place a pinch of mixed Jezebel and Cleo May Sachet Powder in each corner of the room.

MISS CAT'S WORKING GIRLS' LAUNDRY TRICK

"To increase your sexual stamina, encourage reciprocal energy from your clients, and to receive good tips, tie a Dixie John root and Mace arils in a muslin bag and place it in the washing machine with the bedding and underwear that you will use with a client. Once the bedding and underwear are washed and dried, sprinkle a little Cleo May Sachet Powder on them. Use these fixed fabrics to make up your bed and dress in when with clients."

SPELLS TO GET BACK MONEY OWED

One way to get more money flowing towards us is to make sure that any money we lend out comes back to us. If there are unpaid debts floating around out there, you can use conjure to bring those payments home.

TO GET A LAGGARDLY DEBTOR TO PAY WHAT IS OWED
In 1925, Ed Murphy, a well-respected root doctor in Columbus, Mississippi, told Newbell Niles Puckett how he worked for clients to get debts repaid: "Drive five eight-penny nails and four ten-penny nails in the form of a cross into a tree in front of the debtor's house." I like the idea of shouting Ecclesiastes 5:5 as you drive each nail: *"Better is it that thou shouldest not vow, than that thou shouldest vow and not pay!"*

GREEN DEVIL CANDLE FOR MONEY RETURN
This is Miss Cat's spell. She gives the long form of it in her book, *"The Art of Hoodoo Candle Magic,"* but here is my shorter version:

On a Saturday inscribe the borrower's name and the words, *"GIVE ME MY MONEY!"* on a green devil candle. Write his name 9 times and cross it 9 times with *"GIVE ME MY MONEY!"* Put the paper under an overturned saucer, and put the candle, dressed with Pay Me Oil on top. As the candle burns, speak out loud your demand for your money in your own words and close with the phrase, *"Green Devil, I seek what is rightfully mine!"*

Lift the candle, take out the name paper, and singe it in the flame while commanding, *"Green Devil, until [Name] repays the debt he owes, compel him to feel the sting of his conscience, to burn with the fire of remorse. to taste in his mouth only ashes, to dream of the evil he has done, and to remember his debt to me."* Snuff the candle out. Repeat this for seven nights.

Contact your debtor during this week and ask for your money. Wear Pay Me Oil when you do so. If the debt is repaid, thank the Green Devil for his aid. However, if the debt is not repaid, on the eighth night, light the candle and say, *"Green Devil, compel [Name] to run through the flames of Hell until he falls to the ground at my feet with his arms outstretched and the money in his hand, begging me to take it! Now, pay me the money you owe me [Name]! Pay it or burn!"* And burn his name paper up.

Spells for the Wealthy Way

Now that you know how to draw money and how to keep it, the next step is to increase it until you are living the good life — the wealthy way.

CROWN OF SUCCESS SPELL
Begin with a cleansing bath, such as 13 Herb Bath Mix or Van Van Bath Crystals, but mix into it some Money Herbs Mixture or Gambler's Gold Hand Wash. Arise before sunrise, take the cleansing bath, wash downward. Drain the water, keeping a small cup behind, and air dry. Take the left-over water to a crossroads and toss it over your shoulder as you face East.

Inscribe the word *"success"* nine times around a yellow 6 inch candle in a spiral, from top to bottom. Dress the candle with Crown of Success Oil as you state your desire, followed by, "May all my works be crowned with success." Place a dressed lodestone under your incense brazier and in it light Magnet Incense and Money Herbs on a charcoal. Then light the candle.

As the incense and candle burn, anoint yourself with the oil, starting with your hands and fingers, then your forehead, and, last, the crown of your head. Allow the candle to burn down until the first of the *"success"* words that you inscribed is melted, then snuff it out. The next night, light more Magnet Incense, re-light the candle, pray again for your success, and anoint yourself. Let it burn until the second inscribed *"success"* is consumed.

After nine days the spell is done. If you wish to repeat it, start again with a bath and a new candle, as at the beginning.

MADAME PAMITA'S POT OF BASIL FOR PROSPERITY
"When you find coins on the street, save three of them to start this spell.

"Buy a plant pot that is green, yellow, or gold. Prepare it with potting soil and plant Basil seeds. Place the coins in the soil vertically, with one edge sticking out of the soil. Pray that as the Basil grows, your abundance will grow. Water and care for the plant.

"Cook with the Basil, drink Basil tea, or use it to wash your hands or make a prosperity floor wash. As you find new coins, harvest the old ones and replace them. Spend the harvested coins on items from your luxury wish list, or scatter them 'in the wild' for someone else to find for luck.

"Keep the plant healthy and alive, and your prosperity will thrive."

THREE TIPS ON HOW TO HANDLE YOUR PURSE

Here are some valuable secrets from Aura Laforest's *"Women's Work"*:

"The purse in which you carry your money is more than just a place to carry cash; it is a place where money-magic is generated.

- Never set your purse down on the floor or your money will go down; instead, hold it on your lap, hang it up, or set it in a chair or on a table.
- If you keep an empty purse in your closet without a single coin in it, it will gradually go "dead" and lose its power to draw money to you.
- If you give a purse or a wallet as a gift, it is a friendly gesture to put at least a penny in it so it will be lucky for the recipient."

A DOLLAR BILL FOR THE WEALTHY WAY

Miss Cat says that this spell can bring in true prosperity, including ownership of property and time off to spend earned income as you wish:

"On the back of a dollar bill, write this verse of Deuteronomy 28:8: *"The Lord shall command the blessing upon thee in thy storehouses, and in all that thou settest thine hand unto; and he shall bless thee in the land which the Lord thy God giveth thee."* On the front of the dollar bill write your first and last names. Place them under a plate.

"Inscribe your name on a green offertory candle and dress it with Wealthy Way Oil. Burn it for a few minutes every evening when you come home from work. Drip oil on the wick each time you light it.

"After five days of work, you are ready for your weekend, so come home and put five drops of oil on the dollar bill — at the corners and center. Then light the money on fire and burn it to ashes. Rub the ashes on the soles of your shoes, let the candle burn to the socket, and go out and have a good time. You've earned it!"

SECOND PENTACLE OF JUPITER FOR LUXURIOUS LIVING

Wrap a small High John the Conqueror Root, a silver Mercury dime, and a Lucky Hand Root in a copy of the Second Pentacle of Jupiter (*"for acquiring glory, honours, dignities, riches, and all kinds of good, together with great tranquillity of mind"*). Sew this tightly into a piece of green flannel. Dress it with Hoyt's Cologne. It can bring success in any area of life — when you gamble, go for a job interview, apply for a loan, buy luxury goods, or purchase a home. It can be used at any time to bring you wealth. Keep it well hidden, feed it regularly, and it will serve you well.

TO OBTAIN SUCCESS

The mysterious *"Black and White Magic of Marie Laveau,"* ostensibly written by the pseudonymous Bivins, N. D. P., was published in the 1920s in New Orleans and has been in print ever since. The actual author is unknown. It cannot have been Marie Laveau, who died long before it was published, but there is some evidence that points to Helen Pitkin Scherz, a novelist who was married to a New Orleans conjure shop pharmacist, as the writer who transcribed the middle portion of the text, which seems to consist of consultations with a popular African-American seance medium and Spiritualist who was located in the town of Algiers, Louisiana.

The spells in this old hoodoo grimoire take the fascinating form of a client's question to the worker, followed by her maternal, comforting advice and magical instructions. I hope you enjoy this brief look at how to obtain success, 1920s-style. If you like it, pick up the book — it's a classic:

"Oh, dear Mother, I come unto you to ask for your help. My mind and my spirit have been burdened to the breaking point. I beg of thee, oh dear Mother, to turn no deaf ears to my supplications, that I may be successful in those things which I desire within the bounds of reason."

"My dear child, I understand your tribulations and your trials. In order that you may accomplish the desires of your heart, you should start by burning for one hour each day two candles, one green and one red, side-by-side. In front of these candles you should stand and recite the 23rd Psalm one time, leaving the candles to burn the remainder of the hour.

"Dust your body daily with Algiers Powder and anoint your head daily also with Success Oil. Pour one half teaspoonful of Dragon's Blood Bath into your bath water, together with 10 drops of Special Oil No. 20.

"Do these things, my dear child, with faith and constancy, and the spirit of success will smile at you. God bless you. So be it."

A MOJO FOR CROWNED SUCCESS AND WEALTH

Make a mojo in a green cloth bag with a Lucky Hand Root, Five Finger Grass, a small pair of dice, a lucky coin, an Alligator tooth, a Rabbit foot, and a High John the Conqueror Root that has been dressed in Crown of Success Oil. Add something of your own body, such as a hair or fingernails. Breathe into the bag, tie it closed, smoke the mojo in Crown of Success Incense, and feed it a splash of Crown Royal whiskey. Carry it for luck, money, success, and recognition of your leadership abilities.

FREQUENTLY ASKED QUESTIONS

The Lucky Mojo Forum was begun in 2008. Averaging 60 posts per day, it is an online community in which questions are answered daily about the practice of hoodoo and the use of Lucky Mojo spiritual supplies. The Forum is open to all, and anyone can join and ask questions. The Lucky Mojo Forum can be accessed online at:

Forum.LuckyMojo.com

Answers to questions, be they in the form of advice, encouragement, clarification, or spell suggestions, are provided by both forum members and a dedicated team of moderators who are all graduates of Catherine Yronwode's Hoodoo Rootwork Correspondence Course.

Read more about the Hoodoo Rootwork Correspondence Course at:

LuckyMojo.com/mojocourse.html

The Frequently Asked Questions and the answers that follow have been selected from the voluminous body of information on the Forum regarding traditional hoodoo practices and is intended to complete and augment the information that is included in the preceding pages. Here you will find answers to some of the most commonly asked questions in the forum about money and wealth-getting spells. If a question you have regarding prosperity work hasn't been answered yet, it hopefully will be by the time you reach the end of this book.

When reading the answers to the questions provided, note that usernames followed by an (M) are people who are or were at one time forum moderators. Those marked (M, AIRR) are moderators who are also in professional practice as members of the Association of Independent Readers and Rootworkers:

Catherine Yronwode	**Miss Michæle**	**ConjureMan Ali**
Miss Phœnix	**Aura Laforest**	**Devi Spring**

These AIRR members can be reached for personal readings, magical coaching, candle services, and custom spell-casting at the AIRR web site:

ReadersAndRootworkers.org

• Do I need a reading before starting money spells?

Is it required to get a reading first when working on getting a job?
— Unknown09

A reading is not mandatory if you do your own spells, but some workers require you get a reading with them before they will take your case because it helps them to determine the most effective methods for your situation.
— Miss Bri (M)

• Is it morally okay to do money spells?

I was always under the impression it was unlucky to pray for money or to use magic for financial gain. I don't feel right praying for money.
— johnny_gg

If we can pray for other things we want or need, why would that exclude money? What gives money a special category? It sounds like you are worried about being greedy or taking what you don't deserve, but don't we all deserve to be comfortable, successful, and happy?
— Miss Phœnix (M, AIRR)

Doing magic for money is perfectly fine. Money is a tool that can be used to get out of debt, pay for things you and your family need, give to worthy causes, and invest. It is not greedy to want to get ahead in life.
— Mama Micki (M)

• How long must I keep my money drawing candles going?

How long before I need to perform another candle ritual to keep my money flowing? Will I always have to light a new candle after one finishes?
— openminded

You may keep vigil candles or fixed oil lamps going continuously, but not all money spells employ flame. For example, lodestone altars are wonderful, and mojo bags are also an alternative to carry on you wherever you go.
— Aura Laforest (M, AIRR)

• Can I use multiple oils on one candle?

Can I dress a money drawing vigil candle with multiple oils?
— openminded

You can certainly dress a vigil candle with multiple oils and herbs. See LuckyMojo.com/oilblends.html for some suggested blends.
— Miss Michæle (M, AIRR)

How do I inscribe a candle with my petition?

Should I carve my name on top of the vigil candle?
— openminded

You can poke holes in the top of a vigil light or inscribe it. Free-standing candles are inscribed down the sides, often in a spiral, like a barber pole.
— Aura Laforest (M, AIRR)

• Should I clean my candle dressing tool between spells?

The coffin nail I use to carve candles has wax residue on it. Would I want to employ a nail used on a black candle to carve a red or green candle?
— sephirah

This may vary from practitioner to practitioner. Some may pray over a new tool, to bless it, and then cleanse it between each job. Some might feel it is important to have clean tools for each new job, while some may keep their tools as they are in the belief that each work will add strength to the tool. Some do not even think that such things are of any importance at all.

Personally, I clean my coffin nail with a dry cloth. I don't use cold water or incense on such a nail, because this may cut off the spirit attached to it. I wipe it off, and a dash of whiskey keeps the spirit strong between each work.

It's also a good idea to take coffin nails out to the graveyard and leave them stuck in the ground there overnight to refresh them once a year or so, depending on how much work you do with them. I advise you to decide for yourself which way feels most sincere and "right" for you, and to stick to it.
— Dr. Johannes (M)

• Do I need personal concerns from a judge or caseworker?

If I do a sweetening spell on a judge do I really need his hair?
— Random1

When it comes to a business or legal case, we really do not need to get all intimate on the people we are trying to sweeten. A piece of handwriting is fine. Their signatures are, of course, the central expressions of their selves, so signatures are always good to use. Failing that, photos or business cards provide a form of contact. Their names written on paper will also do.
— catherineyronwode (M, AIRR)

• How can I get my money from a government agency?

I have an arrears settlement in child support that will be coming in, but unfortunately the state will be taking it, and I do need that money because I'm currently unemployed. Are there any spells that can stop child support arrears being taken by the state? I'm in need of that money.
— Peels

This is a tough one, because you are up against a powerful, multi-person entity, the state, and you want standard state rules bent in your favour. Personally, I consider it a very long shot, but if you want to try, I suggest you use a combination of Pay Me and Money Stay With Me Sachet Powders, or, alternatively, Money Herbs Mixture. Dust this on all copies of paperwork you have been given or sent by mail, or that you can print out from the internet. Take the dusted papers and a dollar bill — write your prayer on the dollar bill, either in your own words or by using portions of Psalms 35 and 23 — and place them underneath a Pay Me Candle. Set the candle to burn completely before the expected date of the money's arrival.
— catherineyronwode (M, AIRR)

I would add that you might want to petition Saint Jude. You have a lot against you in this situation, so adding some spiritual assistance could help shift things in your favour. You might also want to add your name to the prayer list of the Crystal Silence League at CrystalSilenceLeague.org.
— Miss Phœnix (M, AIRR)

• Can I do money spells if I don't carry cash?

My husband and I almost never carry cash so we aren't tempted to spend it. Many traditional money spells call for coins or currency. Could we maybe anoint our debit cards with oil and place them under a lodestone?
— LilCassandra

You might want to consider doing traditional work the traditional way, with cash. Many financial advisors tell people who are trying to reduce debt to make a weekly budget for themselves and then withdraw that amount of cash. When you see the little pile of cash that you have to use, and know that you cannot spend more once it is gone, it's actually a great motivator for spending more wisely. If you're just dealing with little plastic cards, it's all too easy to over-spend. A budget and cash dressed with Money Stay With Me products may really help reduce spending.
— Devi Spring (M, AIRR)

I agree with Devi on this one. Working spells as they have been done traditionally is worth considering. But not all money spells use money.

Dissolve Money Stay With Me Bath Crystals into your laundry wash water, particularly the socks and underwear load. Use Money Stay With Me Sachet Powder to dust the insoles of your shoes. Wealthy Way products may be used the same way to help your overall financial situation.

Performing a house cleaning with a Money House Blessing scrub can make your home environment inviting to prosperity. This work is not only about money in your pocket, but about your state of mind as well.
— Aura Laforest (M, AIRR)

I wouldn't oil my debit cards because I wouldn't want them to feel oily! However, rubbing Money Drawing, Money Stay With Me, and Wealthy Way Oils into your wallet while you pray is a great plan. It makes no difference whether the wallet holds cash or plastic, you're basically fixing your whole wallet as a mojo for money drawing and keeping. Make up a very small packet with powdered Sassafras, Alkanet, and Allspice, and slip that in. Dress the wallet with the aforesaid oils and pray strongly over it. This is a simple piece of magic that can really help in tough economic times.
— Turnsteel

BIBLIOGRAPHY

AIDA, Miss. *Cursing and Crossing*. Lucky Mojo Curio Co., 2017.

AIDA, Miss. *Destroying Relationships*. Lucky Mojo Curio Co., 2018.

ARMAND, Khi. *Deliverance!*. Missionary Independent Spiritual Church, 2015.

BERRY, Jason. *The Spirit of Black Hawk*. University Press of Mississippi, 1998.

BIVINS, N. D. P. (attrib. to Marie Laveau) *The Life and Works of Marie Laveau*. n.p., n.d. *(pre-1927)*. *Marie Laveau's Old and New Black and White Magic*. Fulton Religious Supply, n.d. (c. 1963); Dorene Publishing (c. 1970). *Black and White Magic of Marie Laveau*. International Imports, 1991; Indio Products, 1998.

CUNNINGHAM, Scott. *Cunningham's Encyclopedia of Magical Herbs*. Llewellyn, 1994.

DE CLAREMONT, Lewis. *Legends of Incense, Herb, and Oil Magic*. Oracle Publishing Co., 1936; restored edition, Lucky Mojo Curio Co., 2016.

FORTUNE, Dion. *Applied Magic*. Samuel Weiser, 2000.

FOXWOOD, Orion. *The Candle and the Crossroads*. Weiser Books 2012.

GAMACHE, Henri. *The Master Book of Candle Burning*. Sheldon Publications, 1942.

GÅRDBÄCK, Johannes. *Trolldom: Spells and Methods of the Norse Folk Magic Tradition*. Yronwode Institution (YIPPIE), 2015.

HAMILTON, Virginia. *The People Could Fly*. Alfred A. Knopf, 1985.

HURSTON, Zora Neale. *Mules and Men*. Harper Perennial, 1935 - 2008.

HYATT, Harry Middleton. *Hoodoo – Conjuration – Witchcraft – Rootwork*. [Five Vols.] Memoirs of the Alma Egan Hyatt Foundation, 1970–1978.

LAFOREST, AURA. *Hoodoo Spiritual Baths*. Lucky Mojo Curio Co., 2014.

LAFOREST, AURA. *Women's Work*. Lucky Mojo Curio Co., 2017.

LEFÆ, Phœnix. *Hoodoo Shrines and Altars*. Missionary Independent Spiritual Church, 2015.

MICHÆLE, Miss, and Charles Porterfield. *Hoodoo Bible Magic*. Missionary Independent Spiritual Church, 2014.

MILLETT, Deacon. *Hoodoo Honey and Sugar Spells*. Lucky Mojo Curio Co., 2013.

PENCZAK, Christopher. *The Witch's Coin*. Llewellyn Publications, 2009.

PORTERFIELD, Charles. *A Deck of Spells*. Lucky Mojo Curio Co., 2015.

PORTERFIELD, Charles. *The Sporting Life*. Lucky Mojo Curi Co., 2016.

PUCKETT, Newbell Niles. *Folk Beliefs of the Southern Negro*. Univ. of North Carolina, 1926.

TEISH, Luisah. *Jambalaya*. HarperCollins, 1985.

YRONWODE, Catherine, and Mikhail Strabo. *The Art of Hoodoo Candle Magic*. Missionary Independent Spiritual Church, 2013.

YRONWODE, Catherine. *The Art of Making Mojos*. Lucky Mojo Curio Co., 2018.

YRONWODE, Catherine, ed. *The Black Folder*. Missionary Independent Spiritual Church, 2013.

YRONWODE, Catherine. *Hoodoo Herb and Root Magic*. Lucky Mojo Curio Co., 2002.

YRONWODE, Catherine. *Paper in My Shoe*. Lucky Mojo Curio Co., 2015.